Still Believing!

*A grandfather looks back on his Christian
faith and living in a changing society*

Gavin Reid

*This book is dedicated to my
brilliant grandchildren
Siân, Sam, Emily and Tom
and
to their generation*

Foreword

It looks as if I may still make 90! I am not far off and my elder brother made it and is still alive.   What this means is that, to many, I am a thing of the past - and more to the point, my belief in Jesus Christ and all that he stands for is also , for very many, a thing of the past.

In what follows I don't want to argue for this dogged persistence in belief; I simply want to share how it happened and what it means to me.

Very quickly here's who I am.   I was born on the banks of the Clyde and am a proud Scot - except for the fact that my parents moved to London when I was nine and I have lived south of the border ever since.   So I am a proud Scot who happens to love England - it can happen!

My first years were during the Second World War and I well remember heavy air raids, flying bombs and rockets. My teens were in the exciting years as Britain gathered strength from its war efforts.   Going to a nearby school, which happened to be a Church of England school, I was drawn into a lively local parish church.   From Sunday School through Youth Club I met good friends (including my best friend who agreed to marry me).   Things led me to offering for the Ministry and in due course I was ordained. Two curacies and eight years through religious publishing led me to a job of leading and setting up missions and advising churches how they might better reach out to those who were not of their number. (I hasten to add that my "advice" was simply the passing on of good practice that I had seen elsewhere).

My concern had always been how the good news of Jesus actually got out from the sheltering of churches to those who were outside. That led me to leading two initiatives that brought the American evangelist, Billy Graham, to English cities in the 1980s. This was not because British preachers could not do an effective job, but because Billy Graham could operate at a dimension that broke into media headlines, and whether people attended his meetings or not, the fact of him being there made talk about God easier throughout all sections of our society. Billy made ordinary Christians share their faith. Readers must forgive me if I refer to these initiatives on several occasions.

Meanwhile my best friend, Mary, and I had three children, saw them grow up and find others to love and I got a letter asking me to be a Bishop (the Church of England has a great sense of humour) and after eight years of dressing up and, sadly, sometimes dressing-down, I retired, worked on my golf and waited to die - well, sort of...

How Did It All Start?

I was once asked, by a church where I was due to preach, that I would first "give my testimony". Now that is not the sort of request made to hoary old Bishops - as I now am. I don't think I had been asked to "give my testimony" since I was a keen teenage Christian.

When I was at Theological College, training to be a parson, I had a fellow student who has since become a University professor of theology, who used to parody some of the testimonies that people gave, (I need to stress that he was and always has been a devout and humble believer). He used to say, melodramatically, something like this: 'I used to be deep in depravity and sin, and then, at the age of six... I was gloriously converted!' We would all chuckle at him but the truth is that every now and then one hears people share how faith in Christ transformed them from living in darkness to living in the light, and such stories can often be very moving - although the change rarely takes place 'at the age of six'!

As I contemplated what I would say in my own testimony it was very clear that I had nothing dramatic to report. Indeed when I used to share my testimony as a teenager I think I tarted it up a little. I would point to a date when I certainly made a big decision, but with the perspective of old age I can see there were bigger, even if more gradual, things in play before and after that fourteen year-old "decision".   What follows is roughly what I said to the congregation on the day when I later preached.

There are four people behind the fact that I have become a Christian.   The first was my father.   The longer I live the more I can see the part he played.   He was not a regular churchgoer although he grew up in a home where his father led the church choir and was the local church school headmaster.   My earliest memories of childhood was of him kneeling, each day, beside my bed, and encouraging me to say a prayer to my other father - God.   I don't think he ever said a prayer for me.   Perhaps in the early days he did, but by the time when my memories cut in, he clearly expected me to know what I had to do.   Words were not said out loud - if I remember correctly - but spoken in my thoughts.   And most of my praying has been that way ever since.

It was from my father that I grew up with a sure quietness that there was a God.   I can remember the shock when, as a boy of about nine, I met another boy who did not share my view.

As I look back I can now see that the second person behind the faith I now have was Hermann Goring - now that is a surprise!   He was the head of the Nazi German air force - the Luftwaffe.   In 1941 he sent his bombers to blitz my home town of Greenock, where many warships could be found, where there were world famous shipyards who were flat out on war effort, and where there was an important torpedo factory.   It was also a place where many thousands lived - including my family.   The Greenock blitz was nothing compared to the blitz on London.   It was concentrated on two nights. On the third night the people of the town were encouraged to trek out and camp on the moors outside, and I can well remember that trek. It was of little purpose because the Luftwaffe did not return a third time.

In those two nights, however, Goring's 350 bombers killed 271 people - many children - 10,200 were injured, 5,000 houses were completely destroyed and a further 25,000 were damaged.   My house had a basement and we all sheltered there.   I can remember, on the second night as the sirens sounded "all clear" I opened the side door and it seemed that from one horizon to another there was a sea of flames.   I was six years old and I had known the fear of death.   In comfortable modern societies many grow to old age having never gone through times when they were face to face with dying - but I had known such a time. As the war continued and I later moved to London there were further times when Goring's bombers and later flying bombs brought that fear back but not to the same degree. On those two nights in Greenock I prayed to the God my father told me was "there" and I continued to do so until the war ended. Looking back, it seemed that I was asking to be kept alive; I was asking for help from whoever was there.

Dying, however, is the surest fact of life and the truth is that the culture I live in gives very little thought to it. There is great thought about sex education - usually left to school teachers - but no thought about death education. A doctor friend of mine once said that most of his patients were kidding themselves that they were immortal.

The third person in the story of my faith was a Sunday School teacher in the South London parish where I ended up as a nine year old boy.   He was not my first memory of Sunday School. For a brief time in Greenock my parents took us to one of the town's Kirks. This suited my mother as she was Presbyterian and that was Scotland's established church. I have few memories and none particularly exciting. I think all ages started together as we all focussed on a man dressed in a black gown in a high and central pulpit. At some stage the children left for their meeting (I think we went downstairs) and all I can remember is getting (or not getting) Bible picture stamps to put in our attendance books.

My South London experience was very different. Seventy or eighty of us (I later learnt there had been an earlier "sitting" in the morning) crowded together in a smallish but pleasant hall. We were led by what we felt was a delightful grandfatherly man who was accompanied by his adult son. I later learnt that the leader was a top businessman who, with his son, was leading a company greatly assisting the nation's war efforts. We just knew him as "Mr Dick". We were encouraged to sing tuneful choruses about God the Father, and Jesus and the cross, about "the best book to read is the Bible" and about following Jesus in daily life. This was all new to me. I never missed, and Mr Dick found excuses to keep me on his team as I grew up and later, and still before 20, I was asked to lead sessions. By that time we were in a bigger hall and the numbers were up to 150. We didn't break into smaller groups - one addressed them as a whole. Armed with a microphone one tried to hold attention, and I think I learned more about public speaking in Mr Dick's Sunday School than anywhere else!

It was at that Sunday School, as a boy, that I saw something of the love and kindness of the God I believed in, and I certainly saw the attractiveness of Jesus and the life to which all of us are being called. I saw it in the Bible stories being told - and I saw it in Mr Dick and his son.

Years later Mr Dick retired from his job and his son took the opportunity to leave the company also and to go to Tanganyika as a missionary teacher. The old man (he had been long widowed) went with him and started another Sunday School. He became so well known that a Bishop who has served in Tanganyika told me that if you wrote "Mr Dick, Tanganyika" on an envelope - it would get there!

Years later again, in Canterbury Cathedral I was about to be consecrated a Bishop. Other Bishops gathered and at the last minute a visiting African Bishop from Tanzania arrived to take part in the ceremony. (Tanganyika had been renamed Tanzania) "Young" Mr Dick was in the congregation. At the reception afterwards the two were greeting each other as old friends and then I learnt that the Tanzanian bishop had also been someone who had learned about Jesus from "dear old Mr Dick".

I shall always thank God for that man and so will Mary, my wife, who was also in the Sunday School.

Then there is a fourth man in my story. He was small, fit and grew up in inner South London. He came from a working class home but in childhood had been helped to his Christian faith through students working in a Bermondsey settlement. While serving In the Second World War he studied to be an accountant and when I first met him he had not then passed all his exams - but he, Charlie Cope, was an achiever. In spite of having a young family and with professional qualifications still to be attained, Charlie was persuaded to start a youth group and Bible Class in our South London church. When I was old enough (13) to join it, that group was buzzing and much of the buzz and fun came from its leader.

Many of those I knew from my earlier Sunday School days were there, which included Mary who later married me but in those days was more interested in horses and the senior sections of the Girl Guides. (I used to joke that she didn't have to buy uniforms, she simply stitched together all her various achievement badges and that more than covered her.)

We would meet one midweek evening for games and on Sunday afternoon for Bible Class followed by tea. We were known as the JKO - the Junior King's Own - a name together with the elder section the King's Own was to be found in a number of churches in those days. I shudder often at the persona I presented at that time. Like other males in my family I was a humourist (or tried to be) and getting a giggle going was something I enjoyed - alas not always in appropriate places. It may well be that I liked to attract attention. On one occasion, however, on a Sunday afternoon Bible Class, Charlie felt I had gone too far. He stopped what he was saying and simply said: "Gavin out. And don't hang around outside!"

The impact on my fourteen year old self was shattering. I had to get up and go out in front of the thirty or more others as an object of disgrace. Also, at another level, I who was a helper in the Church's large Sunday School felt ashamed of being judged to be flippant at a meeting focussing on Jesus Christ. What was also clear, however, was that this was not a rejection. Charlie expected to see me again, indeed wanted to see me again - so I was back for the next midweek meeting and all was forgotten at his end;

but not mine.

That rebuke was what I needed. I needed to be clear that Jesus had to be more than someone I took for granted but someone who wanted to be first place in my life. That wasn't easy and still in my latter years I still need to be reminded of that. God is not an insurance policy against death and Jesus was more than the lead- line in some of my Sunday School choruses. When Jesus first walked up to the fishermen on the Sea of Galilee he didn't say "think about me occasionally", he said "Follow me" and he expected what he got - they left their nets and boats and, literally, followed him.

A few days after this unfortunate episode our church had a youth weekend with three sessions led by a visiting speaker. I went. The man was an attractive speaker but his subject was not. In all three sessions he spoke about *death.* If I remember rightly, he talked about two deaths. The first was physical death and for the Christian that led to a fuller life with the heavenly father. The second death was spiritual death which was the future for those who wanted in this life to have nothing to do with the heavenly father. The speaker spoke three times and always drawing our attention, but his theme was always the same.

Jesus once said "...*don't be afraid of those who want to kill your body; they cannot do anything more to you after that. But I will tell you whom to fear. Fear God who has the power to kill you and then throw you into hell. Yes, he's the one to fear.*"(Luke 12.5NLT)

I don't think our speaker talked about hell or quoted that verse. What he did for me was to underline that believing in Jesus and trying to follow him was the most important thing I could do, and it really was a matter of life and death - and even eternity.

So I owe my faith more to these four people than to anyone else. To put it another way, the Holy Spirit worked through those people as he can and does for others even if they never realised it. (Clearly Hermann Goring did not want me to believe as a result of his wicked plans, but I believe God has a way of working through people in spite of who they are.)

On that Sunday when I "gave my testimony" to that congregation I was speaking to the converted. Their minds clicked as mine did. To very many others what I said, and have written would cut no ice. They might say that I have described how, as a child and a youth in a protected environment, I was conditioned. They might point out that I was never sufficiently exposed to other interpretations of life - let alone God. They might add that there was little intellectual examination taking place. I was being carried along by some attractive people in the middle of a community who thought as they did.

They might add that if chance had allowed me to be born in a Muslim culture, the same dynamics would have turned me into a Muslim; and quite frankly, it is hard to argue with such an observation.

Very few people, however, live out their lives based on studied intellectual conclusions as to what "reality" is all about. Many of those who might challenge me about my faith are challenging because of the way they also have been conditioned. The truth is that we are community animals and most of us never escape the general view of life that is shared by the community in which we feel most at home.   I remember, when I was in my late twenties and involved in a student mission.   One evening I took part in a pretty long discussion with someone who said he was an atheist.   It was a pleasant discussion but it was still one where arguments were forcefully presented and rebuffed.   After a while a thought occurred to me and I immediately voiced it. He was presenting as someone with clearly formed opinions, but I felt a certain defensiveness behind some of the things he said.   "Are you really being dispassionate about some of the things you are saying" I suggested.   There was a pause and a slight smile.   "No" he said.   "I am not!"   The truth was that he did not want to move away from the position taken up by the people he mixed with.

As community animals we are all conditioned in what we believe.   The issue is not whether we hold those views because of our conditioning.   The issue is whether what we believe - however we got there - *is true!*   Proving "truth" however is not as easy as it might seem - especially when it comes to matters of belief and relationships, rather than concrete matters of observation.   To say "I believe in God" is a matter of faith, but then so is the statement "I don't believe in God".   "Belief" implies that we are in the realm of the ultimately unprovable.   This is not a religious issue in itself.   I can, and do, believe my wife loves me.   If asked for proof I would simply try to spell out what living alongside her has been for me over the years.   That is all I can do and if my answer does not impress the questioner then there is nothing more I can say.

So why do I believe that my belief in God is true?   For me the answer has to be my experience of living with a belief in God over many years.   In the chapters that follow I am going to spell this out, guided by a daily prayer that, for some years, has been part of the first hour of each day. It is a prayer based on what I had heard of a similar prayer used by a Christian leader I have always respected. It is based on three "thankyous" to the Christian belief that God has to be seen in three ways - *the Father, the Son and the Holy Spirit.*

My prayer is, as follows:

> *Thank you Father for wanting me to be*
> *alive and for the gift of this day.*
> *Thank you Jesus, my rescuer and friend*
> *for calling me to follow you,*
> *Thank you Holy Spirit for promising to be*
> *with me throughout this day and*
> *Throughout my life.*

I have come to see that these thank-yous are at the heart of why I am *still believing!*

The Gift Of Life

Thank you Father for wanting me to be alive and for the gift of this day

There are two things that I realised from my earliest days as a child - that I existed and that the world around me of good things and bad, also existed.

"Existence" is a puzzle. I remember talking to a retired academic professor. He was an atheist and while not of the militant tendency, he nevertheless sometimes took on public debates with Christians as to whether there was a God or not. One day I met him after one of those debates and he admitted to me that the previous evening, his opponent totally wrongfooted him with his opening comment. He had started with this question: "*Why is there anything?*" Knowing this man as I did, I am quite sure that he was able to hold his own in reply, but the fact that the question had made him uncomfortable at first, and that he admitted it, was telling. Why indeed is there anything? The sterile argument of creation versus evolution totally begs the more important question of existence itself.

At university I was told that one of Britain's greatest philosophers simply said: "The universe just is. That's all we can say."

The Bible simply bypasses the problem with its first words: "In the beginning God created."

Those words in themselves contain a puzzle. The puzzle is not only "God", but the concept of *beginning.* The human mind cannot easily understand this *beginning.* For us time is all about what is before and what is after. To talk about the beginning of time breaks the very logic of time. What was before the beginning?

The old tale in Genesis does not try to unravel these mysteries, it simply goes on to describe the fact of a Divine being - but that is where, for us, the story starts. The existence of God is not, for me, the issue. The issue is what is this God like. The first clue comes from the next words in the old story. God created. The God described is not content just to "be" in splendid isolation. 'He' wants companionship and for that he has to give life to others. And the summit of his creative activity is mankind - male and female with both fully being the image of their creator. And that "image" must include that his ultimate creations have minds of their own. To be one of many minds in a company is not easy. Loyalty to the creative mind has to be offered, it cannot be demanded or manufactured.

Anyone who is a parent will have to admit that with the joy of parenthood, there are also the trials of living with others who have their own minds about what they want! My wife and I only had to cope with three other lively minds in our family. If the Genesis story is true, then God has had to cope with billions of minds all wanting to express their will on each other. It is small wonder that history has been full of wars and human tensions, but nothing else could be expected following the Creator's decision to create in his own image.

The image of God, however, is the image of a *giver.* In spite of all the conflicts that emerge from a world populated by people who have minds of their own, people are at their noblest when they are driven by wanting to give rather than wanting to get.

The image of God also holds out the prospect of human creativity and compassion, and, yes, goodness.   We are all capable of self will but also self giving. Jesus once said that even in the middle of a world that is full of selfishness, that "the gentle can inherit that earth", and history shows that some of the greatest human achievements have come from gentle people.

The Creator also, through all the complexities of our origins has created a world that is beautiful to our eyes.   In the Garden of Eden version of creation (Genesis has two accounts) we read *"Out of the ground the Lord God made to grow every tree that is pleasant to the sight and good for food.."* (Gen 2.9NRSV). It is within the gift of those created in God's image that they can perceive and produce what is beautiful.   In Christianity, and indeed in other religions, artists have been called into play to express human feelings about God and his creation.   That ability to create what is beautiful extends beyond religion.

And into this world that exhibits, and can give rise to, beauty and generosity; we self-willed human beings have to live out our lives; and that living is part of the gift of God's creation. Every day is a gift and every person is a gift. If there is a creator God behind all that is, then my life is not an accident.   Quite simply; I am meant to be, and that can be said of every person we meet.

To think like this is not only to find value in myself but also to see value in everyone else.

There are some words that St Paul used to some of the first

believers. *"For we are God's masterpiece. He has created us anew in Christ Jesus , so that we can do the good things he planned for us long ago."(Eph.2.10 NLT)* He believed that those who follow Jesus become the sorts of people that God already wanted us to be before we caved- in to self-will. Paul believed that God had good things in mind for us to be and do, and all we have to do is to discover them, or in some cases let them discover us! As an elderly person those words are an encouragement to me. If I wake up in the morning then there are still things where God can use me. Every day is a gift from God and, indeed, I myself am meant to be a gift from God - although that thought is, perhaps, kept to oneself!

For the Christian then, every day is a gift from God. That said, it does not always seem so. Some days seem to be tedious and even when one wants to do the right thing for God, the right thing does not always seem to crop up. One of the words in the Bible that is rarely thought about is the word, *waiting.* Years ago I was due to travel overnight from a northern station to London. I had booked into a sleeper and when I arrived at the station I was shown to a parked railway compartment, all by itself at the platform. It felt quite odd, and even more so as I got into my pyjamas and sidled into bed. Halfway through the night, the train arrived from Scotland and there was a jolt as my carriage was attached. I needed to wait for the connection to continue my journey. And as God has to juggle with all the myriads of people's intentions and movements, those who want to walk in his way may have to spend times waiting for the right connection. And those times could well be baffling to figure out.

Some years ago I travelled to several of the places where St

Paul had travelled. One of them was called Troas. That reminded me of a baffling time in St Paul's life. A time of waiting, and I think he wasn't a very patient man. He had set out, with a small group of others, to share his message about Christ in various parts of what is now Turkey. Somehow nothing seemed to go right. The account of this journey says that in every direction that he intended to go the Holy Spirit said "no". We don't know what exactly occurred, but Paul reluctantly had to pull away. The result was he was left in this place Troas, once an important seaport but by Paul's time somewhat run down. All that lay ahead was the sea.

And Troas was where the connection happened. In the space of a day he had met a Macedonian doctor who was awaiting a passage back to his home country, and he had a vivid dream. In the dream Paul felt he was spoken to by a Macedonian man (did he look like that doctor, I wonder?), and the man said "come over to Macedonia and help us!" When Paul woke up he went straight to the docks and joined the doctor on his trip back to Macedonia. That was where God wanted him to go in the first place, and the Macedonian doctor, Luke by name, became his first Macedonian convert and a friend for life.

In the course of my life I have never applied for a job with success. Either circumstances changed and the application fell through, or I failed. That said, doors opened to me that I never sought and they proved to be doors that opened into very fulfilling passages of my life. Mary often said to me that when one applies for jobs we should thank God for the doors that close as well as the doors that open. God is not only the one who gives us life, he is also the one who walks with us - more of that anon. Jesus once said *"I will not abandon you as orphans".(John14.18 NLT)*

Believing in the "Father" God that Jesus talked about means far more than assenting to a philosophical proposition. It means seeing oneself as a wanted son or daughter. It also means that our heavenly Father has plans for our lives. Like every child we can decide to go our own ways - most people do - but meaningfully or accidentally we can go through the doors that God wants us to go through, and that leads us to a better way for each one of us. That better way, however, is not better just for us, but better for others also.

In the 1980s I was involved in an invitation to the renowned American evangelist Billy Graham. At first we were only a few. The tide of opinion in the British churches was not with us at first and the general public - if they had any views on such matters - assumed an American evangelist was someone who played on emotions and ended up wealthy as a result.

Billy and his team were well aware of the British church's mood and needed a lot of persuasion. The sort of large scale evangelistic missions they held required immense local agreement and participation. Our small group got an agreement from the Graham organisation that if we could show there was strong support for the project we had in mind then Billy would consider it. That began strong lobbying to church leaders and especially to Bishops. I remember one Bishop saying he would be happy to talk but the only time he had available was the journey from London to Reading on one particular evening. I volunteered to be his chauffeur and when he stepped out of the car he promised me his support!

After many months we felt that we had our level of support and the Evangelist said "yes". And this is the point, *I felt that my job was done.* I had always been an ideas man and I assumed that I could go back to my normal job. Not so. The American team felt that those who had campaigned for the project must be seen to be leading the project. That thought had never occurred to me, but I found myself with the grand title of "National Director" having been seconded by my then organisation for two years. Two years later with over a million people attending the meetings with thousands more meeting for video sub-gatherings and several national television programmes, 4,750 local churches involved and 96,982 people making some sort of a Christian commitment, the phrase that ran through my mind was that we "had stumbled across a bit of God's agenda".

I didn't realise it at the time, but it showed that God could use me to run this sort of operation (although I was joined by some very able people who provided wisdom, technical expertise and financial skills). Until that project my experience of leadership was to lead a small church in Essex and a number of youth camps! Operating, later on, as a bishop, was to operate on a much smaller scale! And yet the whole story was really what God did through someone who had been given the ability to come up with ideas! (I also have to add, as I look back, that not all of my bright ideas have proved to be that successful!)

I once met a frail elderly lady who was committed to Christ. She lived on her own in a small house near Liverpool. She was limited in her mobility but she saw that the time this gave her was a gift from God. She prayed. And when I say she prayed, I mean that she parcelled out long portions of each day and armed with literature from different Christian missions and causes, she had a routine to work through and she prayed. When someone took me to see her she was asked "what part of the world are you in today?" I think she said "South America".

Every one of us, I believe, has gifts. For me, dare I say it, my main gift is the sort of imagination that throws up ideas. As I look back I can see that happening in my childhood and in youth club days when I dreamed up daft ideas and some sensible ones.   Thinking up ideas, however, is not the same as knowing what to do with them. I needed good logistics people to make them work.   I remember saying to a business executive friend of mine that I was not really good at being number one in an organisation. He replied that I was as long as I had a good number two!

The elderly lady in Liverpool had the wisdom to see time on her hands as opportunities to pray.   Some might have felt that she, in her infirmity, was locked in. She saw it as a chance to be locked on.   God's gifts, I believe, are not only about inner abilities but also about outward opportunities.

Perhaps the most important gift and opportunity all of us have is to the planet which is our home. Long before people dreamt up words like 'ecology' and 'environmentalism' the old creation story in the Bible made it quite clear where men and women were to be directing their concerns. *"The Lord God placed the man in the Garden of Eden to tend and watch over it"(Gen 2.15 NLT)*   In my lifetime humanity has come to realise that the future of the planet,- at least for humanity to flourish, depends on the way we live in it. The old text calls the planet 'a garden' but the danger is that a careless humanity could turn it into a wilderness.

All these ideas that the world and everyone in it was meant to be, and that every day is a gift, and that each one of us has gifts to offer, and that our greatest responsibility is to service the planet which in turn services us; *come from a belief that there is a fatherly God behind all that is.* At the heart of our word *faith* are the letters *A* and *I*. For me, faith is all about acting *as if* what I believe is true. Believing is not a state of mind or simply the arrangement of propositions in my head, it is about *living* in the light of those propositions and expecting them to prove to be true.

I remember, many years ago, opening a letter from Canada and reading that someone I had never met knew about my role in the large evangelistic mission with Billy Graham and asked if I could come to a group of ministers in Toronto and talk about it. He gave his phone number and he mentioned a particular date. That date was free so I phoned. It was a pleasant voice on the other end and I said I was willing to go but what was I to do? He told me that he would arrange for a ticket to be held at the Air Canada desk in Heathrow Airport and all I had to do was to go there and give my name and all would be well. I was given, a day or so later, the time of the flight and when the day came I set out - not totally sure that this was not some hoax! I got to the airport desk, gave my name, and a smiling attendant handed me the ticket! Why ever did I doubt? What I did was to act as if I had been told the truth and the truth vindicated itself. For me, faith in God has been like that.

And yes, in my old age I can look back on moments when I had times when I could have doubted, but such times have not lasted very long and subsequent events often gave them meaning. The truth is that after all these years I am still believing.

The Call To Follow

Thank you Jesus my rescuer and friend for calling me to follow

It starts on page 1165 in my copy of the Bible but that page, for me, is where the story really begins. It describes when the local carpenter in a small town called Capernaum emerged as the man who changed history. His name was Jesus. For several years since his father had died he had been running the family carpentry business and apprenticing his younger brothers to take over, and they would have to, because he had known from childhood that he had a different path to tread. We will never know how much he realised who he truly was in his childhood and teenage years. We are not told, and I am not sure how much he himself knew of all that lay ahead, but we know that as a child he was once found talking with religious leaders in the temple in Jerusalem; and was very clear that the God they talked about was, he felt, his true father.

So, on page 1165, I read that this thirty or so year old left his workshop and went down to the shore of the Sea of Galilee and approached a group of people who he almost certainly knew - a group who earned their living by fishing - and he put a simple proposition to them. He simply said "Follow me!" And they did!

Of course we in our times know a great deal of what happened in history and what didn't. There almost certainly were not King Arthur and the Knights of the Round Table. Some have said that Jesus, likewise, was a figure more of imagination than fact. The evidence, however, for a man named Jesus, operating in what we call the first century in the Roman province of Judea, is unchallengeable by any test of the historicity of a human being's existence. The historical documents that mention Jesus that have survived from those times and in the two centuries afterwards, are the best attested compared to any other figure of that period. There is more literary evidence of the existence of Jesus than there is of the existence of Julius Caesar.

Whether what those documents record is true is another matter, and here one has to look to other ways of making judgements and beliefs. I believe that Jesus lived and that it is wise to take the records about him as credible. Others do not. Those others cannot prove they are right and neither can I. *What I can do is to live as if those records are true and see what happens in my life, and look at the world around me with eyes shaped by those beliefs.*

I return therefore to those words Jesus said to the fishermen on the shores of the Sea of Galilee - "follow me". For them it was a call to leave their boats and tackle and to trek around in support of a remarkable figure. The theme that Jesus lived by and wanted his followers to live by was *the Kingdom of God.* The concept of Kingdom was a big issue in the occupied Judea of their day. They wanted Caesar and his legions out and a new king of their own blood to reign. The Romans knew this and had puppet kings in place, like Herod, who had Jewish blood in their veins but who took their orders from the Roman Governor.

Jesus, however, was thinking at a different level. He did not think that people should live, first and foremost, as subjects to a human ruler, but to the rule of the Heavenly Father from whom all of us came and to whom all of us must answer. He knew that societies must respect their political leaders if there is to be any semblance of order, but that we should live as if God is the only one who is in charge. This first priority could, at times, make his followers out of step with their fellows and their rulers. Supremely this was demonstrated in the first century, with the crucifixion of Jesus himself .

For those first followers the task was simple. They had a physical person calling them to walk and live alongside him, and that is what they did. To follow Jesus over twenty centuries later is quite another matter. We live at the end of a long history of developing, and often, arguing different Christian traditions. Even in a godly cause, human nature intrudes and sometimes in unhelpful ways. As we saw earlier, humans being made in God's image can lead to the freedoms of different minds clashing with each other - we are not compliant robots. So we now have labels and differences - catholic, protestant, orthodox and within them further labels such as anglican, methodist, baptist and so forth. And there are subdivisions within the subdivisions - evangelical, charismatic, fundamentalist and so it goes on.

The trouble from all these complications and rivalries is that the call to "follow Jesus" works out in different ways with different expectations and even different languages, and sometimes even gets lost. To quote the old saying "we cannot see the wood for the trees". Perhaps the biggest complication is the way we use and understand the word "church".

Most people think of a building when they hear the word "church". It is common to say that people "go to church" or don't. Any priest that gets appointed to be the Vicar in the Church of England (and in most other denominations) has a building to look after - and if that building is historic it means a great deal of looking after. A congregation at any church will soon find that money and time has to be raised to maintain the building. And many of our church buildings are magnificent and many in our congregations - and indeed, outside - find great peace in these buildings. That said, the great danger about how we talk about "church" is that we think in static rather than dynamic terms. Following Jesus becomes the membership of a club. The buildings where Christians meet become shrines rather than temporary shelters.

The word for "church" in the Greek language used in the original accounts of Jesus and his followers is *ekklesia.* It is far from static. It certainly does not relate to a building. It means people called together for a purpose. You don't 'go to it' you belong to it, sharing it's cause.

I once heard a story of the renowned Kate Booth, the fiery daughter of William Booth, founder of the Salvation Army. Her exploits made her quite a celebrity and on one occasion she was invited to a prestigious gathering. A Civil Servant was asked to greet her on arrival and escort her until the meeting began. Faced with this renowned Christian leader - as she had become - he tried to find an opening for a conversation. He said something like "I go to church", to which she replied "Is that the best you can do for a dying world?" Her reply was more than a put-down. It revealed that the "church" is meant to be people who challenge by their ways and their words the society that surrounds them. Jesus once said *'I am the way'* and his first followers were widely known in their society as *'people of the way'*. Following Jesus makes you different. St Peter writing to scattered groups of Christians described them as *"God's chosen people who are living as foreigners"* in their societies.

For me Peter's description of being the church, being christian, has become clearer the longer I have lived. The Britain in which I was a child had a strongly Christian feel to it. The churches were not necessarily full, but there were plenty of them. Christianity was on the curriculum of state schools and had a special place. Sunday Schools run by the churches reached out to the majority of the nation's children - and even if most people seemed to graduate out of that children's religion, a high portion of the population knew the story of Jesus Christ and their values were affected by that story. As a boy and a youth I did not feel that I was a foreigner in British society. Now I do. St Paul talked about making one's aim to "please God" but my society encourages me to please myself. One cosmetics advert encourages those affected to buy their products because "you're worth it!"

It is not an accident that "worship" and "worth it" sound similar - they come from the same root. The cosmetics advertisement is calling women to worship themselves. If they buy the product it is because it will enhance their appearances and make them feel better about themselves - at least that is the promise. The truth is that should someone buy the product it is the seller and manufacturer who will be enhanced. The western world may have moved away from its acknowledgement of God (in England census returns show that in the years 2001 to 2021 those who claimed to be Christian fell from just under 72% to just over 46%) but the reality is that people remain worshippers. It is just that we now worship ourselves, or our cars or our reputations or our smartphones, or our favourite football clubs or our clothes or whatever. Bob Dylan once had a song where the repeated phrase was "You gonna have to serve somebody". That is a song about worship, about who or to what you give worth.

I once met somebody who, as an adult, became a committed Christian. At the time when this happened he was working for a high powered consultancy firm. Affected by his new faith he reassessed how he calculated his business expenses and began to put in significantly lower claims than before. The trouble was that this new honesty showed up the practices of his partners - they were all putting in exaggerated claims. He was asked to leave. It was a clash between someone who was trying to serve God and a group who wanted to serve themselves.

Years ago my wife was acting as dinner-lady at a local school and got on well with the other dinner-ladies. A time came, however, when she wanted a day off to attend a meeting where I was speaking. Her colleagues simply said "put in a sickie!" She felt this would be dishonest and applied for the day off. She got her day off but she was also "sent to Coventry" by her colleagues. Her attempt to do what she thought was right showed up the wrong in her colleagues, and they didn't like that. When Jesus was living in Judea most of the tensions he created were that he showed up what was wrong in those around him simply by his life and character, rather than his words.

So how do Christians in today's world actually "follow Jesus" - and in cases like mine, how do children and young people do so.   As I have said, I grew up in a home where my parents were clearly, and willingly, part of a Christian culture.   It was shown in that they encouraged me to pray, they taught that there was right and wrong, they would not tolerate swearing and encouraged me to be caring with regard to others.   They were comfortable within Christian worship but, when I was young, were rarely in attendance.

Their culture was the prevailing culture in the years when I was growing up.   Schools taught scripture as part of the curriculum and had daily assemblies when hymns would be sung and the Bible read.   I was not conscious that my values as someone wanting to follow Jesus clashed very much with those around me.   My path was made easier because I belonged to a church youth group which was well attended and this all helped me to feel that I was in the mainstream of my society.

There were times at school when I was aware of "dirty stories" and as I grew older I, as with all of my generation, would begin to feel sexual attraction towards girls.   My membership of a mixed youth fellowship where we were all friends, however, subtly encouraged me to see girls as friends more than "girl-friends".   This meant that while romances and marriages came out of that fellowship over the years, those marriages were based on friendships and to the best of my knowledge none of those marriages ever broke down.

Somehow or other, however, my identity as a Christian in my school seemed to register with others, and there was one day when this came home to me.   Every day a prefect was expected to read the Bible lesson at assembly.   We would be appointed to do this on a weekly rota.   One week the prefect doing the readings did not do it with much enthusiasm, and it showed. Half way through the week before the assembly I was stopped by the Deputy Head and told that the Headmaster had asked for me to take over at fifteen minutes notice. It was not the best day for me as I was very bothered about the fact that after the assembly I had to sit a retake of a Latin examination which I needed to pass to take up my University place - and I was bad at Latin!

The assembly started and I went forward to read the passage fixed for the day. It came from some words Jesus said as recorded in John's Gospel. And this is what I read to the school:

"If ye abide in me and my words abide in you, ye shall ask what ye will, and it shall be done unto you..."

I don't know what those words meant to the hundreds of schoolboys in front of me, but as I sat down after reading... God knows what I was thinking!

All through my writing of these words I have been painfully aware of the difference between what it was like for me as a Christian at a day school and what it is like today. The Christian boy or girl goes to a school locked in today's questioning and sceptical culture. They go to school where very few of the teachers or the other pupils feel part of a Christian culture. They go to school with a generation where everyone is locked into a music culture which has strong sexual undertones, and where love is sex more than sex is a component within love. They go to school where the dominant educational role is often played more from what comes through their smartphones than from their teachers.   I am aware that some of those who come from church-going families need a great deal of courage to declare it.

Again in my three years at London University as a day student I faced little difficulty in being known as a Christian - indeed in 1954 when Billy Graham was preaching for three months in London, I had little difficulty in filling a bus with other students to go and hear him. It was not until I had to undergo two years in National Service that I faced any challenges - and even then not to a great extent.. A key moment was my first night in a barrack room. I knew that I would have to kneel by my bed to say my prayers. When the time came I did so although my mind was full of what others might think rather than saying very much to my heavenly Father! There were no comments from others, perhaps even a greater silence. When I got into bed and it was Lights Out I became hugely aware that the Father I had tried to pray to was saying "well done!" I have never forgotten that experience. Nor have I forgotten that the next morning there was that same silence in the barrack room and up at the far end another recruit was kneeling by his bed. When he finished he crossed himself. I as an evangelical and he as a Roman Catholic were on the same team. Whatever may be our differences, and some are profound, those who own up to Jesus before others are the same team in God's eyes.

National Service - I was in the Royal Air Force and served as an Educational Officer - was a good experience even if I wished, at times, I could get the two years over as soon as possible. I soon struck up a relationship with the chaplain at my station which was a recruit training base. As he was a crack pistol shot and required to take part in various competitions, I ended up as a sort of reserve chaplain and several times I took chaplain's hour speaking to several hundred recruits who were both bolshy and weary from hours of square-bashing. After that sort of experience, preaching to a cathedral full of worshippers was far less daunting! I served in a department with about six or seven others and we got on well. There was, however, one moment which made me reflect on how much my witness was being blunted with the full engagement in group cheerfulness. One of my colleagues was talking one day about something - I think in the news - that spoke about Christian enthusiasts trying to convert people. He smiled at me and said: "Of course you don't believe in conversion do you?" I cannot remember what I replied but I hope it made clear that I do!

The main challenge to my following Jesus was living in a world where sexual innuendos within people's language were commonplace and swear words were sometimes built into what were virtually technical terms. St Paul talked about our minds and the renewing of them as a result of belief in Jesus. This renewing is partly the work of the Holy Spirit - but only partly. He wrote, in his letter to the Romans: "*Don't copy the behaviour and customs of this world, but let God transform you into a new person by changing the way you think.*"*(Romans 12.2 NLT)* God transforms but we have to actively want this by "changing the way we think".

My National Service was followed by two years at Theological College. They were, in the main, happy years but there were tensions and some of these were caused by the shades of theological positions within the student body - even in a college clearly within one overall tradition. It is not hard to see that there were tensions within Christ's followers even when he was among them. We should not be surprised to encounter them today. Some of these tensions come from people's egos, but some come from people's determination to stick to what they believe to be right in God's eyes. Being "cooped up" in residential communities is not always easy. David Watson, a much admired contemporary of mine, who sadly died too soon, once created an extended "family" around him. Many admired him for this and asked how it was to live in this "ideal" way. His reply was "difficult".

What I learned from the college experience is that human nature will always intrude into attempts to be a Christian community. St Paul talked about the constant tug- of war between the "old nature" and the "new". This tug-of-war, he said, goes on within each person's life so we must not expect it to disappear when we live closely together. It was during my time at college that I got married to my closest friend. It was a joyous experience and has been in the over sixty years that followed - but it has never been devoid of moments of tension!

So to my first curacy in East London and, of course, by this time I had a clerical collar round my neck. That fact made me different from others in the business of following Jesus. I was now being paid to name the name of Jesus. Others would expect me to do that so in some ways it became easier for me to name that name. Those who were not identified with Christian ministry would not have that advantage, and to name the name would take far more courage. Again as a clergyman many of the settings for my witness to Jesus would be set up in my favour. It is easy to talk of Jesus from the pulpit in a church. It is far more difficult to do that to others in a secular setting.

I remember preaching in 'my' East London church about witnessing to Jesus at work. At the end of the service a member of the congregation, who worked at Fords in Dagenham, sought me out and arranged a meeting with him later in the week. We met at his home and he carefully pointed out what it was like to work on a conveyor- belt setting. He pointed out that one's pay depended on keeping the line moving, and that meant the same for his work-mates. "There is no way we can talk about our faith in that sort of setting," he said.

One of the dangers of people working full time in Christian ministry is that we can become remote to the actual realities of life for most people, and our advice becomes irrelevant. Further, words about Christ spoken out of the blue to people - because we feel that we should be saying such words - can fall, as Jesus said, like pearls before swine. A favourite saying of his was "those who have ears to hear, let him hear." The job of Christians living in a world that is often alien to their way of thinking, is to live in such a way that people may find that they do have "ears to hear". I once heard Eddie Stride, a down-to-earth minister in the East End of London, tell a story about two men who worked together and who got on well in each other's company. One day one of them admitted to the other that he had been to an evangelistic meeting and had decided to become a Christian. The other replied "I've been wanting that to happen to you - I've been a Christian since my teens!"

The first took a moment and then said "I've been thinking about it before, but I've always noticed that you seemed to be very happy in your life so I thought you didn't need to believe in order to be happy! I wish you had owned up earlier!" Whether we work on conveyor-belts or otherwise, if we form friendships there will be settings when we can own up to our faith at appropriate moments - and we should pray for those moments.

The first followers of Jesus were unlike any that came thereafter. They had Jesus with them and there were no existing churches to bind up their time in fundraising for buildings or whatever! We cannot follow Jesus as they did, but we can learn from the dynamics of what Jesus did with them.

Jesus was a carpenter. He had learnt his trade from his father. In the times that he was with us, trades ran in families. His first followers were fishermen because their fathers had taught them the trade. Jesus had several brothers and it would appear that his father had died before he was thirty - maybe earlier. He would have had to teach the trade to them as his father had done with him. He had learnt his trade through being an apprentice. That was the usual way people learnt. When it came to training his first followers he used the apprenticeship method. He asked his followers to leave their former ways of life - at least for a while - and live alongside him and watch him ministering to others. That is a very different way of learning than from going to a theological college! Before very long he would send them out to do and say the same as he had been doing.

Today's new or aspiring Christians need to start with a "dose"of Jesus! He may not be physically present but in the gospels we have what his first followers wanted us to have - a "dose" of the man they had lived with. When we read early in the book of the Acts of the Apostles that a large number of people wanted to join the ranks of the first church we read that *All the believers devoted themselves to the Apostles teaching".* The qualifications for being an Apostle were spelled out earlier in the book when the first followers wanted a new recruit. They said they were looking for that new recruit from *"men who were with us the entire time we were travelling with the Lord Jesus....Whoever is chosen will join us as a witness of Jesus' resurrection."* Acts 1.22,23 NLT)

When I reflect on these words I cannot avoid comparing it with what we would cover when we took Confirmation classes, or even in courses like the much used and blessed *Alpha* courses. I really do not think that we immerse ourselves enough in the gospel accounts of Jesus. Too often what we "teach" (and that word needs some reappraisal) is a bit of Jesus, a bit about the Church and its traditions and the place of the Bible. If I were starting again I think I would try to start with, and try to stay with, Jesus - the stories about him and the things he said.

When Britain, like many other countries, imposed shut-downs on its citizens during the height of the Covid crisis, I tried to write a book. I had talked with a publisher, just before I retired, about writing a book about following Jesus. The trouble was that this was some twenty years earlier! I wanted to contrast what it was like to follow Jesus when he was calling his first disciples, and what it was like to be a follower today. I never got around to it and as no contracts had ever been signed, the whole thing lapsed. When the Covid crisis hit us I was well into my 80s and hardly an author for another publisher to take seriously - but the trouble was I still wanted to write that book. So - I did!

In that book I had tried to suggest how we could do the next best thing to living alongside Jesus as had the first followers. I suggested that we read the gospel stories and in particular, took careful note of The prayer Jesus gave to his followers, the Beatitudes which spelled out the values of those who believed that God was the true King of all, and the Last Supper when Jesus took an old tradition and changed it to spell out that he was like broken bread for the sake of others and that those who shared in that broken bread were family, were forgiven and looked forward to an eternal banquet in a better world. The story built into that Last Supper was what Jesus wanted to be at the centre of our understanding about him.

I suggested that the stories and sayings of Jesus were like case law, suggesting how we respond to situations that we might face. There is a verse in Paul's letter to the Ephesians that spells out, I believe, what this is all about. The best translation is to be found in the New Revised Version - which follows the Authorised Version. Faced with wrongful ways of living, Paul writes *"That is not how you learned Christ"(Ephes.4.20)*. Our job as Christians is to learn Christ - not just *about* him, but trying to enter his very personality. Of course we will fail, but what a great challenge throughout one's life.

My book argued that the churches were weakening in numbers and getting elderly overall. The two factors that preserved Christianity in the last hundred years or so were the strength of local churches and the influence of Christian parents. My own story showed how churches could gather in children, hold many as teenagers and be replenished by new generations of young adults in their congregations. That is no longer the case. The churches of fifty years ago - and I was a minister then - could rely on plenty of young adults being at least partly aware of the Christian story - and told to them by people who believed in that story. Evangelism was helping people to start trusting what they already knew. I remember discussing this with the evangelist Billy Graham. He told me that he was, in most cases, finishing off what had already been started. That sort of evangelism is no longer what is needed. We have to start earlier and spell out the story of Jesus, and that requires working in much smaller dimensions than great stadium meetings. The format of the *Alpha Group* is nearer the mark for today but much has to happen before a person would commit to joining any sort of group that relates to the Christian faith.

That is why, in the book I wrote during the Covid shut-down, I said that Christians needed to become what those first Christians who operated in an alien society were called - *people of the way.* We had to learn Christ so much that we stood out as those who had found a better way to live. And that way of living required us to be outgoing and caring, and to be ready to give a reason to others as to why we live like this.

To return to my own story of trying to be a follower of Jesus. I now can see that I learned Christ not so much through being a student, but by being a practitioner. Yes, Sunday School and Bible class and Confirmation groups and listening to some pretty good sermons, all taught me a great deal, but not as much as having to teach Sunday Schools in my teenage years, and to being part of "Witness Teams" that went out to other church youth groups, and to leading and sharing in Bible Study groups with those of my own age on our Youth Group holidays. That pattern was not too far from the way Christ's first disciples learned their faith and it can only be how the first churches took hold - and spread.

In the Church of England's approach to doing things, there is one way where we do follow the apprenticeship model.

On ordination a minister starts as an "Assistant Curate". In the days when there were more clergy around one did - as I had to do - two curacies. Of course it was expected that we would minister to others and earn our pay - but the main reason for these assistant curacies was that we should be apprenticed to someone who would train us for ministry ahead. Some of my contemporaries were not as well served as I was - but as one of them said "you can learn from failures as well as successes!"

As I have mentioned earlier the shape of my ministry was not in the classic Anglican mode of moving from one parish to another. I served two curacies and then was invited to join an organisation that served parishes with various levels of support. It was called the *Church Pastoral Aid Society* (CPAS). My job was to develop a new publishing arm for its work. Their leader, Timothy Dudley-Smith had started this and was looking for someone to build on his work. (I was not the first person he approached!)

For five years I worked on booklets, books and the occasional filmstrip. I wrote my first book, which my boss was not too happy about at first! I networked and developed a wide circle of mainly young talented people - mostly of my generation. I enjoyed publishing but I was not honest enough with myself to realise that I enjoyed publishing, but only as a string to my bow - there were other strings, and in particular a call to be involved in evangelism. Strangely enough, very few people are "converted" through books and booklets, and those who buy Christian books are usually (surprise, surprise!) Christians already.

Back in my teenage days I went to a weekend conference with other members of my church, and on Sunday, I and a few others, went to the local church for the early morning communion service. As we waited for the service to begin we were the only ones there. In the end only about two or three locals joined us. Until that time I had belonged to a very well attended church and I suppose I thought that was what all churches were like. The emptiness of this church shook me, and as I reflected on this I seemed to "hear" some words. The words were: *what are you going to do about this?*". I mentioned earlier that there was nothing dramatic about my "conversion" - but this was dramatic. I went into that church as a fairly carefree teenager who wanted to be a vet or a journalist (with a secret longing to be a racing driver!) and I left, feeling called to Christian ministry - and that call has never left me.

In spite of that very clear "string to my bow" I was nevertheless head hunted by another religious publishing organisation, with a long and famous record, to become their religious editor. My book on christian communication, *The Gagging of God* had just been published and in my little world I had a certain amount of fame! I was flattered to be offered the job and I accepted it but with too little thought. The change of jobs meant that the family had to move and because I was a priest and expected, in time, to go back to a parish vicarage, the organisation bought me a house. So the family moved and within a week or so I realised I had made the wrong decision.

For nearly three years I tried to do the job but I found the bigger market I was expected to serve was more difficult. Looking back I can now see that the whole market for religious books was shrinking, but many of my problems came from my own failings. That experience taught me something that many people have to face. I had to do a job I did not like simply to feed my family. Eventually a way was opened that enabled me to go back to my former organisation for a new job that was tailor made to fit that call I received as a teenager in that virtually empty rural church. My new job was called *Secretary for Evangelism* as it was my task to try to help parishes to be more effective in sharing the good news of Jesus - which is not easy.

For several years I travelled around England visiting parishes, listening and talking with clergy, learning how to advise on evangelism and church growth and setting up missions - usually for others to lead but sometimes accepting the lead myself. I found that few clergy had been trained at college on evangelism. It seemed that no-one had ever taught principles and practice. Our colleges turned out professionals at theology (albeit at various levels) but amateurs at evangelism. For many clergy who longed to see people turning to Christ, the model in mind was the sudden conversion of Paul on the Damascus road, rather than the gradual conversion of Peter and the rest of the disciples. I began to point out that when one analysed the story of most Christians, they had come to faith not through a crisis but as the result of a process. I conducted a quasi survey with almost every group I met which revealed, on almost every occasion, that they had come to faith through relationships and over time - parents, friends or links to an attractive Christian grouping.

What I also saw was that most people's embrace of the Christian faith was sealed before they were through their teens. Children's work - often left to elderly ladies or groups of teens - was where evangelism actually happened. The trouble was that the Sunday School - to which I owed so much - was dying out all across the country. Sunday had become a multiple-choice day for families and it only took a few years before we were moving into generations of young parents who had very little relationship with churches.

In the 1970s however there were still churches reaching and holding teenagers, perhaps not to the degree of the 1950s when I was young, but there was plenty to keep one encouraged. However this was the period when the so called charismatic movement was affecting much of what went on. It often tended to encourage groups and churches to look more inwardly. It brought in an emphasis on informal worship which in turn fitted in well with the guitar music where most of our young people felt at home. It talked about people being "filled with the Holy Spirit". It is hard to be critical about such developments - we all need to worship and we all need the Holy Spirit. What I felt with all these new emphases was that they might go hand-in-hand with a move away from the need to share the gospel with those outside of one's Christian groups.

Whether I was right or not, those thoughts led me to setting up young people's meetings in London for several years in the early spring. I had in mind what the British evangelist Tom Rees used to do when I myself had been a teenager. We would choose four Friday evenings in February and March, initially in the Friends Meeting House and later in All Souls Langham Place. We called them "Meeting House" after the first venue and the name stuck. Our meetings had four components. We would be led in congregational hymn singing, we would have a speaker who spoke to some particular theme (the first, I remember, was on Christianity and other faiths) and then, after an interval, we had a mini-concert, originally from Garth

Hewitt, and finally I would speak on a gospel theme and close with an appeal. We drew about 300 or so on the first meeting but the word got about and 500 to 600 were at the final meeting of the first series.

Although my own church in Surrey used to bring in a coachload, most of the people came from smaller churches by cars and public transport. There was a great buzz at those first meetings and I made it a point to wander round at the intervals and talk with people. The last thing I wanted was to be some sort of "star" player. One person who came revealed he had the equipment to print enamel button badges and soon people were sporting these "Meet me at Meeting House" badges.

I shall always remember one night in the second series with about 800 present in All Souls church. The visiting speaker in the first half spoke on the theme of "spiritual warfare" opening up the fact that being a Christian meant that one had to take sides and that opposition would come not just from other people but Satan himself. I am well aware that this sort of subject could be handled in an over-alarming way but our speaker, Roger Forster, presented his case with great care. He had hardly finished when the building's fire alarm went off and I was told to clear the church. My heart sank as I saw all those youngsters streaming out. The experts went to work and there was no fire, only some freak happening with the alarm.

I remember feeling the dismay that everyone had gone, only to find out that they had not! They were all outside, hundreds of them! In they came and we carried on. We had hardly started when a music stand simply went flying across the floor. By this time my rational mind began to wonder whether something other than normal was happening. I began to speak and soon after the fire alarm went off again.   It was a chilling moment but this time I knew what to say. I said "we are staying!" and a great cheer went up all round! None of us got burned and to this day I have never been sure that we were not on the receiving end of a number of freak happenings or whether the dark enemy had been at work.

My concern to reach teenagers with the gospel led me to write a confirmation book - surprisingly called "*To be Confirmed*",   It actually sold about 100,000 copies which was way out of my league as an author - but then churches would buy the book in bulk for their teenage candidates. Alas as I write today there would be poorer sales for such a book, first because books are not the way to engage young minds; and there are far fewer teenagers seeking confirmation.

The other thing that became clear to me in the 1980s was that the heart of any church youth group was formed by youngsters who had graduated up from Sunday Schools. After the collapse of the Sunday Schools in the sixties and seventies it seemed to me that the churches had to find new ways of reaching children, and there were some good examples to be found. At that time I had become a member of General Synod and a report came out from the Board of Education (the Church of England Synod has "Boards" that cover certain areas just as Parliament has "Ministries"). The report was about ministry to children, but it was clear that it was only about children already within our ranks. I moved an amendment that we needed another report to see how we could become better at reaching new children. My amendment was passed and I ended up on a group working on this. I drafted the report which was called "*All*

God's Children?" which not only argued that the churches were failing to reach children but other less worthy influences were. The report was debated and passed with only one vote against - and like so many such reports, very little happened as a result.

By the time I had become a Bishop in a largely rural diocese few churches had children's work and even fewer had work amongst teenagers.

I was made a Bishop in 1992 as a junior to the Archbishop of Canterbury in his diocese and I found the task very fulfilling and very tiring!   As the years followed I became very aware that we were coming up to the end of the century and the year 2000 marked a moment when we might alert our wider society about Jesus Christ.   Our calender was dated as "AD" - the latin words relating to being after the Lord's birth.   I felt that, as with bringing in Billy Graham in the 1980s, this was a chance to bring mini-middle and mega societies together in one theme.   I was also aware that the Government were planning to mark the turn of the century with large scale celebrations and there was talk of "the Millenium Dome".

As a junior to the Archbishop I talked about the Church getting in on the Government act and he, George Carey, was very enthusiastic.   I found myself heading a new committee charged with making something happen!   I went to see the Government minister in charge of the forthcoming celebrations and she had the head of the Millennium Commission with her.   I asked how much the Government had realised that the millennium was really a Christian celebration and that there was no other rational for celebrating it.   Her reply was "What an interesting thought!"

She was far from cool as to what I was saying but her first reaction was to say that if the Government took that route it might offend other faiths.   I had come across this call to avoid slighting other faiths before.   I went back to Church House and asked if I could meet some leading figures of other faiths and a meeting was arranged.   When it took place I reported on my meeting with the Government minister and what she had said.   There were smiles all round.   A Jewish leader said "we have our festivals why can't you have yours?"   I think they could all see the ploy behind appeals to other faiths.   The ploy is to neutralise all talk about faiths altogether.   At our meeting the Muslim Imam said "the battle today is not between those of us who believe but with those who don't".

I left that meeting with ample proof that, while other faiths did not want to be marginalised, they were in support of playing up the place of Jesus in any Millennium celebrations.   One of those present, the Sikh leader Indarjit Singh scrapped two of his BBC "Thought for the Day" slots and spoke instead of the place of Jesus in the Millennium.

That start led to three years of bringing the Churches together into a central committee, negotiations with the Millennium Commission to ensure that Jesus was featured in their famous "Dome" and trying to galvanise the churches at local level to come on board to link the year 2000AD with the name of Jesus Christ.   It was a time of ups and downs and I fear the tensions got to me from time to time.   At one stage I found myself representing the whole Anglican Communion at the Vatican to compare notes with what the Roman Catholic Church was doing.   At another stage I was packed off to Geneva to engage with the World

Council of Churches on the matter, only to find that when I got to the hotel there was a telegram waiting for me from the President of the Palestinians reminding me of the importance of Bethlehem in the story of Jesus!

I retired towards the end of the millennial year 2000 feeling that our efforts, while not a failure, could have been better. It is very hard to try to rally all the Christians in Great Britain to do anything together - but at least we tried. The Government put me on the New Year's honours list for my efforts. When I went to be invested with my medal the Queen said I had been through a "busy year". I remember saying that I thought my task was to tell the nation about the meaning of the Millennium but the bigger task was to tell that to the churches!

I soon found that, when I retired, the Church and its organisations had a low view on the importance of old people. I was a has-been. When I talked to several other retired clergy I found that they felt 'out of the loop' and, at most, objects of pastoral care rather than being seen as offering pastoral possibilities, let alone being strategic. Twenty years later, however, that is no longer true. The Church of England could not survive without the ministry of its retired clergy - especially in rural areas. And one thing about being a retired clergyperson is that I am not involved in Church politics and controversies. People look to us simply to be a minister! In my second decade of being retired I had led a church through its Rector's well earned sabbatical and then at 81 led the same congregation for a year after he left. That was followed immediately by leading another church (actually two that worked together) for over another year. I loved it and there are many retired clergy who have had similar challenges. The day will come when our cultures (the Church and the Nation) will recognise the value of elders - as many third-world countries have long done.

Coming back to active ministry after being detached for so many years has taught me how much more challenging it is to be a Christian minister in today's world. It also showed me a little of how it is to minister in a society with few roots to the faith. I will mention two things that stood out to me - one serious and one less so.

The first relates to marriage or partnerships and their children. I remember speaking in a debate in General Synod, in 1992, on Cohabitation. A motion had been put up which clearly wanted everyone firmly to condemn the growing practice. I took the phrase "living in sin" and asked where the sin was. The Bible defined marriage as a man leaving his parents and joining with a woman openly and living together. I suggested that this was exactly what many if not most cohabitations were all about. Yes there were a good number of what might be called extended fornication arrangements, but for very many the relationships were meant to be permanent.

One indication of this permanence, in an age of family planning and abortions, is the production of children. When I had to give a pastoral lead at 81 I had to face unmarried couples asking for their children to be baptised. I believe some clergy refuse but it seemed to me that the child mattered and that the church has got to catch up with the reality of marriage in the twenty-first century. I developed a patter when I visited the couple. I would say that I wanted to baptise the child but that would mean that the child would now enter the family of the church and that would mean that, as a church leader, I had a responsibility to the child. I needed to ask what guarantee I would have that the parents would stay together until the child reached adulthood. It became very clear that I wanted an answer. I often found that the father had never considered that but the mother had! I pointed out that unless there was a recognised marriage there could be problems for the child if the couple parted. I didn't press church weddings. It was a great joy to me, however, when two of the four or five couples I dealt with came back and asked to be married.

One of the issues that affect people is that some feel they cannot afford to enter into the rat race that now entangles marriage, with its stag and hen parties and elaborate weddings and reception arrangements. One couple I met saved for two years to arrange a residential wedding for many guests, only to go and stay with their in-laws afterwards. I have sometimes heard the phrase "the wedding industry". Couples are expected to find thousands of pounds to celebrate their marriage - I think, if faced with that, I would cohabit!

The second issue I found was related to weddings. In the light of cohabitations becoming fairly normal, I had to get used to conducting weddings with the bridesmaids or page boys actually being the children of the couple. Again, because most couples knew more about weddings from films than churches, I found that several couples expected the bridesmaids to walk in front of the bride as she came up the aisle. Also they expected the youngest bridesmaid to go first ahead of those taller - which meant that the success of the procession depended on the three-year- old in front actually knowing which way to go. That was not always the case!

On one occasion the bride fell out with her father at short notice and asked her brother to 'give her away' - only (thank goodness) to fall back in with her father at the last moment. They agreed that she would be led in by father and brother on either side. All went well at the church door until the small page boy (who happened to be her son) insisted on holding hands with his mum. Thus The Bridal March was played as the four walked, side by side, to the front.

How then can I sum up my life as someone trying to follow Jesus? Have I always been clear as to what I had to do or be - alas no. Have I used all the gifts and opportunities that God has given me - very sadly no. There have, however, been times when I have known that I was doing exactly what God wanted me to do. Marrying Mary was one of them! Trying to be a loving father to my wonderful children, was another. Starting the Meeting House series of young people's evangelistic meetings in central London in the late 1970s was another. No, there were not thousands of youngsters coming - only hundreds; but those hundreds mainly came from small congregations around the city and to gather with so many others of their own age created a buzz and also helped many to discover Christ. At least one present Bishop was one of their number. I loved preaching to them.

Again in the 1970s and early 1980s Mary and I led house parties for youngsters between 12 to 15. Many years later I met one of those who came and who had become a doctor. She told me that those house parties were the happiest holidays that she had ever been on. After she had said this, Mary and I reflected that they were probably the happiest holidays that we had been on as well - in spite of being run ragged keeping seventy or so lively youngsters happy, and safe, and leading a team of helpers. We knew that sharing the gospel and showing love to others was what we were meant to be doing.

And then, of course, there was setting up and leading the great missions that took Billy Graham to seven major cities in the 1980s, with well over a million people attending, and very many making major steps to and into Christian faith. I remember feeling that we had "stumbled across a piece of God's agenda" and that is a very great privilege. That was followed by a further mission in 1989 based around London and televised live to 150 other venues throughout the country - again I felt I was at the centre of God's will.

Yes, there were times when I thought I was doing and being what Jesus was calling me to do. Alas it was not always like that. There were times when I knew I was lost, and times when I went - sometimes knowingly - in the wrong direction. Those were the times when Jesus had to be the Good Shepherd he talked about, who went out to the rescue. I cannot look back to some great initial experience of "being saved" as some Christians can do. What I can say - and this again comes from looking back over a long life - is that there have been many moments when I felt that I was being saved. I am so grateful for that.

Being Accompanied

Thank you Holy Spirit for promising to be with me throughout this day and throughout my life

If there is anything that is clear to me as I look back on my life, it is that I have been accompanied. There is a moment in John's gospel when Jesus forewarns his followers that there will come a time when his physical presence will no longer be with them. Faced with their dismay at hearing this, Jesus continues. *"But in fact, it is best for you that I go away, because if I don't, the Advocate won't come" (Jn 16.7 NLT)*

The word John uses in Greek is a word that is difficult to translate in one word of English. Many versions use this word 'advocate', some use 'comforter' and some 'helper' and some 'counsellor'. The Greek word means *someone called to be alongside.* One of its uses was for a defending counsel in court. Jesus could never be alongside everybody as long as he was himself a physical body. The very spirit of Jesus, however, could be with millions of people at the same time.

My present car has a sat-nav. When I plug in where I want to go a voice comes over the speakers telling when a road junction is ahead and where I have to go. If there was only one person who could tell me that then no one else could have the same guidance. In fact everyone who has a sat nav can get the same guidance. The Spirit of God, of course, is no inanimate device, but he is the way Jesus can still be with everyone who wants to follow him.. As John also records: *"No I will not abandon you as orphans - I will come to you.' (Jn 14.18 NLT)*

For many Christians the thought of the Holy Spirit is associated with experiences such as speaking in tongues, or prophesying. During the time of my ministry there was a great deal of interest and discussion about such experiences, and certainly in the church of New Testament times such experiences are described. Phrases like *'being filled with the Holy Spirit'* are to be found and this can easily be linked to experience.

I have lived through this period and there have been times (not many) when I have had experiences that seem to fit with others, and seem to reflect the references in the New Testament. That said, I have been concerned that many Christians have been encouraged to seek particular experiences, and this can lead to disappointments when they feel it has not happened. Let me take some occasions when I felt (at the time or later) that the Holy Spirit had made himself felt. I mentioned earlier that moment in a virtually empty church when I seemed to sense a voice saying, with regard to empty churches, 'what are you going to do about it?'. Did I really hear a voice? Could it not be a vivid thought that flashed in my mind? There are no acid tests one can use to measure such things. What I do know is those words changed my life and I believe God was behind that change.

I mentioned earlier also my first night in the barracks when I served in the Air Force. I knelt to pray and when I got into bed I had a tremendous sense of the presence of a fatherly God saying 'Well done!' But that experience could simply be that of someone who believes in God feeling a great sense of relief and interpreting it. There was another occasion when I was staying in a friend's house and I was awakened by a great sense of wind blowing through the room although the curtains were not stirred. And I was praying, but the words coming out of my mouth were not in English. Or could the whole thing have been a vivid dream? The night before I had spoken with my friend about a problem that had distressed me deeply - the tragic death of a friend's child on a houseparty that I was leading. He had listened very carefully and drawing on passages of scripture reassured me that the death had not been my fault. Perhaps my dream was triggered by that. In the midst of the experience was a deep sense of being caught up in the wind that seemed to be blowing through the room. I felt I was being set free and blessed, whether it came from God directly or whether it came from an imaginative semi-conscious dream.

My sense of being accompanied, however, does not rest with these sorts of experiences. It rests with the way things have happened. It has been more with providence than experience.
Again, let me share some moments when I felt the Spirit of God had been at work.

My first story contains a lot of detail but I hope readers will bear with me. At 19 I went to Queen Mary College, London, to read Geography for a BA degree. This required an inter-BA pass in Latin which I did not have, but Queen Mary College was one of the few London Colleges that offered a course in Latin while one studied one's main course. I took Geography as much to please my old school teacher as anything else, because I was actually better at History.

I was quite clear, however, that ordination was what lay ahead and I hoped that after passing my degree and then serving two years national service, I would go on to a theological college. My elder brother was already at such a college.

It was not long before I realised that I had chosen the wrong course and I was doing badly in the subsidiary subject of Geology. It was also a very difficult journey every day to the college from my home. It seemed to me that the best thing was to quit, to do my national service and then do a longer course at theological college, and I knew from my elder brother that at his college they offered an external London BA in Theology, Philosophy and Ethics, which made far more sense for a budding clergyman. I spoke to the head of the Geography department at the college and he said I would have to speak to the Dean of the Faculty of Arts. When I went to see the Dean - I can still remember his name, it was Hatto - I found a very kind and understanding man. He listened to my story and then said (I can still remember his words) "No student of mine should do an external degree when he can do it internally. Quit Geography, stay on and get your Latin, and I will arrange for you to switch to Kings College which offers the same degree." (I could not have gone straight to Kings in the first place from school because I did not have Latin).

I passed my Latin (which is a miracle!) and moved to Kings and in two very happy years I got my degree. I felt that someone was indeed alongside and helping me in all this.

My second story followed shortly after the first. I have mentioned that I was in a lively youth fellowship. What I have not mentioned is that all through my teens I had a real fear that I would end up unmarried. It is odd, but it is true and partly related to the low image I had of myself.

That low image was partly from being the younger brother to what I felt was a more talented elder brother. (I later learnt that he thought I was the more talented!) It was enhanced when, at about twelve, I learnt that I had to wear spectacles. Before I admitted my short sight I learned the bottom line of the eye test board at school which was produced for occasional tests. I can still remember it : ZCOSVXPE! After cheating for a while I realised that I needed to see what was written on the classroom blackboard, so I admitted my need.

Wearing spectacles as children opens one up to a certain amount of ridicule. My wife, Mary, who had to wear glasses as a child, can recall that other children used to throw stones at her on her way back from school. So it was that while I tried to be the great humorist at my youth club, part of that came from a great deal of insecurity. As I moved through my later teens I had one or two girl friends, with very nice people, but usually these relationships simply drifted apart amicably.

For all this time I had known Mary, and her brother, as good friends. I have mentioned earlier that Mary was very much a girl's friend rather than someone who wanted to be on the end of a boy's arm! Our youth club used to go sailing on the Norfolk Broads every year and I became the "Vice Commodore" - which meant I had to draw up the lists of who would sail with who on the various boats from day to day. I always made sure that Mary was on my boat for the last day - she could sail well and was just fun to have around.

As I approached my twenty-first birthday I had sorted out

my daft worries about being wifeless! I was enjoying University and decided that girl friends could wait for another day.

On an April day as our youth group was being driven back from our annual cruise in a hired coach I was wandering around chatting with several others, and ended up sitting on the floor behind the driver talking to Mary who was in one of the front seats. Someone in the row behind Mary (actually it was our Vicar) called out "Mary do you like having boys sitting at your feet?"

"Yes" she said. "Especially when it's Gavin!" She thought it was an amusing answer. I thought it was electric! I suddenly realised that Mary was the person that God wanted to share my life. I am not sure that was how she saw it at the time but within six months she woke up one morning quite convinced that this was what God wanted. Sixty three years later we are still convinced about that!

Some years go by before my next story. I was, by then, a curate in my second parish, serving a church on a housing estate, much of which was built on the former wartime Hornchurch Airfield. I had a small but growing congregation and I was out visiting when I passed what had become a rubbish dump. As I walked by I became aware that there was a wreck of a car and that a young lad was sleeping in it. I went over to him and learnt that his parents had turned him out, and that he was sleeping rough. I told him to go round to the parsonage and tell my wife that I had sent him round for a bath and a bed! He did so and for a couple of weeks became a member of our family. It is a long story and at one stage the police were involved and I had to speak up for him in court. However, in the middle of it all I got him sorted out with his parents and we found him a job as a car mechanic - and this is where the story really begins. He was due to start work on a Monday and had to report with his own socket set. By this time he had started coming to our church youth group and we were all due to go on a sailing weekend on the Friday evening led by a remarkable Christian minister, and he wanted to come.

We started on Friday morning going together to tool shops to get a socket set. By this time his father was in full support and had given him the use of some credit arrangement to help buy the set - this was before credit cards had taken over our lives. We found the sets in various shops, but none of them were into the credit arrangement. Shop after shop said they could not help and time was running out. In the end I fished out my cheque book and bought the set myself - it cost about £14, which was a great deal in the mid-1960s. It certainly was a lot to me because it was about half my bank balance and there were at least a couple of weeks before my next pay-cheque. We would have to feed the four of us for the rest of the month on about £12.

The sailing weekend was a great success although Mary and the children had to stay at home and miss all the fun. However while we were away Mary discovered that our small son Stephen had a letter to me tucked under his pillow. He had begun intercepting letters and not telling us what he had done with them. It was his latest game! When I returned Mary handed me the letter.

It had come from a charity that helped impoverished clergy and which had helped me in the past, but to which I had recently written to say that I was expecting a pay rise and would not need any further help. Their letter in reply thanked me for what I said but they felt I might just need one further gift, and they enclosed a cheque for £30 - just over twice of what I had spent to buy that socket set. I cannot be blamed for thinking that someone "up there" or as Jesus put it, someone "alongside" had been at work. I was being accompanied.

A few months later a letter arrived offering me a job for CPAS, a long established society that supported parish ministry offering grants to to help parishes take on extra staff - in my first parish the society had partly paid my stipend. My letter invited me to develop their new publishing department. Publishing was not something I had planned to do but the job offered new possibilities that matched my interest in writing and finding ways to communicate the gospel. I think the Holy Spirit had been at work, and the invitation came when Mary and our young family (about to have a new addition) needed to have a break from a very demanding parish that expected their minister's wife to be as much "staff" as her husband.

As I have said earlier, after five years I was headhunted by another religious publishing organisation, with many important books in its past, and I was flattered and with too little thought said "yes". My change of jobs came with the death of my father, who lived over a hundred miles away, and as I look back I can see that I was deeply grieving at the time. All the more so because I was asked to take the funeral, and it was attended by my mother, my father's sister, my brother and my wife - and that was all. Even now as I write this, I feel choked that after seventy years of life and a caring attitude to everyone he met, there was no one else to join us at Dad's funeral. In seven years of retirement (when my parents had moved to a new area) and after regular attendances at the parish church, it seems that he had found no friends. Years later I stood up in the pulpit of my own church, and preached the sermon on my Dad that four years earlier no one had come to hear.

My new job in publishing very soon showed me that I had made a mistake. That said I had to do my best because I had moved the family to a new area and I was the breadwinner. For well over two years I soldiered on and then one evening the phone rang. It was a call from my former colleague Eddie Shirass who had taken over my job. We swapped thoughts on what we were doing and in the course of our conversation he mentioned - almost as an afterthought - that my old organisation was looking for a person to fill a new post which I had suggested was needed years earlier. He said there was a joke running through the staff and it was "Come back Gavin, all is forgiven!". We laughed but as I put down the receiver those words were not a joke to me. I phoned back later and said that I was more than willing to be considered.

A move back, however, meant further change for my family and then it all became clear. For my old organisation, CPAS, it was a new post and so they would have to buy a house. For my present organisation it would mean that they would be left with a house to sell. The two contacted each other and a deal was done. The house was sold for £22,000 pounds and I used to joke that I was the only clergyman who had a transfer fee from one charity to another.
When Eddie phoned me did he plan to sound me out for the post or was it a casual comment? It certainly sounded like the latter, but for me it was a real call of God. My heavenly companion was working on my behalf, and it so happened that staying at the old address proved to be a better place

for my family and for me as I faced a life of travelling around the country. I shall always look back to that phone call as an act of God and it certainly changed my life.

I have mentioned earlier about my connection with the American evangelist, Billy Graham. Since his visit to Britain in 1954 when I took a busload of students from my college to hear him,, I had long believed in the value of his ministry. Quite apart from the many thousands who would claim they had been converted through his ministry, his visits in the 1950s and 1960s had a remarkable effect on the numbers of people who went forward to full time Christian ministry. I remember a senior member of the Church of England Board of Ministry saying that Billy Graham was the best recruiting officer that they had - which is not bad for an American Baptist!

In 1969 I wrote that book entitled *The Gagging of God.* It was an attempt to reflect on how the Churches today communicate their message in the world of the later twentieth century. In that book one of the things I wanted to share was the sorts of 'communities' we actually live in. I suggested that geography was not always the context for a community. In suburban society with most people owning cars and relaxing in front of television sets (today ipads, smartphones and laptops would have to be added) people can have very little awareness of what happened with other people in the next street. A church in one road might draw on a large congregation while two streets away no-one would know. I suggested that people live in three different communities. There was, most importantly, the mini-community of family, friends, work colleagues and perhaps a neighbour or two. Then there was, as the second most real community, what I called the mega-community.

Radio, television and the press place each of us in a world where we know more about presidents and film actors and singers than we know about the people living 100 yards from our home. Only as the third most significant community was the geographical region where one lives. (The virtual communities opened up through social media did not then exist)

Of course these are generalisations and in small rural communities and in long-standing urban "villages" the midi-community comes into its own. The local church, however, operates in the midi-community and often has very little impact on the minds of those who often get up in the morning and travel off to work somewhere else, and then come home, tired, shut the door, and turn on the television or sit at laptops.

This is why I championed Billy Graham with his very high profile and large gatherings that cannot help "making news". And the "news" he made was about God in a time when God was being crowded out of public awareness. Billy could not do his work unless churches all banded together in support but when they did those churches nearly always gained in numbers and in commitment to their own mission. I remember hearing of a Bishop who turned up at a Confirmation service a few months after Billy had preached in Bristol. Nearly all the candidates were the results of Billy's mission, and the Bishop called out to the startled congregation: "Three cheers for Billy Graham!"

Billy operated in the mega community, but he was also in the midi and mini communities at the same time. As I was travelling around the country trying to stimulate evangelism at the level of the local church I began to see that we needed something that would reach out beyond midi-communities to make people aware of the Christian agenda. Unlike the USA, British churches had little *direct* entry into television and radio. There were regular religious slots on public service broadcasting in both media, but the editorial decisions rested with the broadcasting corporations rather than by churches, national or local. This was far from bad. It protected British audiences from a rash of ill considered and even exploitative programming. By the 1980s however, religious broadcasting was firmly slotted into certain times and this meant that those who wanted them knew what buttons to push and when, and those who were less disposed avoided such times. Towards the end of the twentieth century and up until the present time the editorial people became more interested in responding to those of other, but growing faiths and to religious controversies. The BBC and the ITV companies saw religions as something to be described rather than something to be promoted.

I looked to Billy to be a news item rather than part of a religious discussion, and (apart from Papal visits) I could see no other person or organisation which could have that effect.

I had only been in my job as an evangelistic advisor for a couple of years before I felt that Britain needed Billy back. However big evangelistic meetings were out of fashion even to those who used to enthusiastically support them. Society at large has a short memory. The days of the mid-fifties when the American evangelist held his great stadium meetings and within a remarkably short time had the media moving from opposition to warm encouragement - all that was forgotten. When Billy came in the mid-sixties there had been a strong degree of hostility towards him from some commentators on TV and the radio. I know that some of what happened hurt him quite deeply.

The evangelical Christians who were usually Graham's greatest supporters were caught up, in the seventies with inner controversies over the charismatic movement, and were increasingly locked into the view that evangelism should be based on the local church and through personal contacts (both of which was true) but saw big campaigns as an extravagance and diluting the efforts from where they were meant to be.

Those in other traditions saw people like Billy as American hot-gospellers making money with little sincerity, and with little understanding of the need to transform society socially as well as spiritually. During the 1970s there were one or two brief attempts and false starts to get an invitation under way but they usually fizzled out fairly quickly. It took two or three of us to quietly but persistently press the case from the sorts of mindset I have just described. We needed not only something that stood a chance of leading people to faith in Christ but also of triggering off national discussion within which churches and individuals could find entry points into closed minds.

As I write this I can see that we are in a long story but at least it might show that my involvement in all this was as someone who tried to think about how we could stimulate evangelism in a society that was almost getting too busy and diverted to think deeply about anything. After several years our group had thought up a plan that brought all my "communities" together. We were to plan three years of stimulating church and personal outreach, with a visit from Billy to several regions of England half way through.   We left London and the South East out and plumped for Bristol and the South West, Birmingham and the midlands, Manchester or Liverpool and the North West and Newcastle and the North East.   Those regions had good regional media but In London media were more national and international and we did not feel he would get good coverage in the capital.   We learnt that Billy was in Southern France in July 1981, visiting his daughter who lived there, and he agreed to spend an afternoon with us in Nice if we could get there.   Five of us did, and we put our ideas to him.   We didn't give him an invitation.   What we did was to outline our plan and say that if we could go back to those regions and seek an invitation of sufficient strength for him to come in that setting; could we say that he would come?   He said, cautiously, "yes!"

It took nearly another year of travelling, holding consultations and, in my case, talking to as many Bishops as would give me time before we could see that we had the groundswell of support that would make him agree to come.   During this period the Bishop of Norwich asked why we were not coming to East Anglia and he virtually convened a consultation on our behalf.

That consultation in a hotel in Norwich still stands in my memory.   It started with the Bishop - who had to go on to other appointments - standing up in front of the scores of local clergy and church big-wigs and making it clear that he wanted Billy to come.   It ended with a moment I shall never forget.   We had arranged to gather for a meal at the hotel to take stock.   Norwich was our last area consultation.   We had with us two members of Billy Graham's staff, one of which was Walter Smythe who was Billy's virtual Foreign

Secretary. He was a man of a quite imposing presence, and I don't think he was totally convinced about our project. After the meeting the hotel had cleared a bedroom and set it up for a meal for about ten of us to take stock. We gathered and a waitress was getting everything sorted out, and then she stopped and addressed us. I am afraid we had been so immersed in ourselves that we had hardly noticed her. I also know that as a Norfolk woman she was probably quite shy. "Do you mind if I say something?" she asked.

We were transfixed! She went on, "I'm glad that Billy Graham is coming here because, years ago. He led me to God!" It took a stunned moment before we thanked her, profusely for speaking out, and I still think there was some moisture in Walter Smythe's eyes. He needed no more persuading, and that young woman may well have brought Billy back to Britain in 1984.

So the project that I had been dreaming about for several years was set to go except that Walter Smythe had one other thing to do. He made it clear to me that I had to be the continuing, up front, leader of what turned out to be a million pound project. In the three years that followed I had to live in a car for much of the time servicing regional committees, overseeing booking six football stadiums, finding team members and central committee people, sleeping in hotels and spare bedrooms, eating in service stations, dealing with strong differences of opinion, and making sure I said the right things to radio and television interviewers. There were days when I woke up with a feeling of dread at what might happen next, and yet I had this sense that I was not alone.

I felt the Spirit's presence particularly when dealing with some of the people I had to try to bring together. At one stage in the project we had to decide whether Billy should preach in Liverpool or Manchester for that stage of the mission. Manchester had some very powerful lay leaders who were giving us strong support and some of them could look back to supporting Billy when he went to Manchester in the 1960s. Liverpool on the other hand had stronger support from the congregations - including many Roman Catholics - and that opened up another can of worms that I had to sort out at a later stage!

At central level we decided that Liverpool was the better stage for the regional part of the mission and I had to go and tell the Manchester leaders - some of whom were managing businesses and used to getting their own way. As I drove up to meet them I was increasingly nervous and when I met them they sat there looking quite formidable. I decided to tell them the truth. I said "To be honest I'm really quite scared of you!" It was obviously the right thing to say! The room fell silent.

"We can't have that laddie!" said one of them - and they all smiled and relaxed. Together we all worked out what we had to do and everything ended well. As I look back I think I can see that another person was in the room.

This sense of being accompanied is a conclusion I have drawn from disappointments as well as apparent successes. Written into my psyche is an expectation of failure which goes back to schooldays. When I was twelve and in the A stream of my school's year four, and early in the autumn term, at the morning registration something happened which I have never forgotten. Into the classroom came the deputy head with a new boy. I was called out, told to clear my desk and in front of all my classmates was escorted out and led to the classroom of the C stream. The new boy then took over my desk. The humiliation of it was crushing and it took me over a year to recover a sense of self respect.

When I was a curate I had been the deputy leader of a series of summer camps for children. In 1961 the leader was standing down and the rest of the team were expecting me to take the lead. A member of the overall organising committee, however, came to me and said that the committee did not have confidence in me for such a role. That was a bitter pill to swallow and it all seemed to go back to the fact that I was known as a humorist. In organisations that extol seriousness, people with a sense of humour are usually not judged to be serious enough. When I was on the short list to become the new Director of the CPAS, where I had served for many years, and where most of my colleagues thought I was a "shoe-in", again I did not get the job and again I felt deep disappointment - only this time I was quick to see that the decision had been a correct one. My organisation needed fresh insights, and a call to be a bishop was just around the corner.

I have said that Mary often used to say to me that when you push at a door and it doesn't open - that is as much divine guidance as when it does. I am sure she was right but, at the time, one does not always see it that way!

My biggest disappointment, however, was one I learned about much later, and I use the word dis-appointment with accuracy. While I was serving as Bishop of Maidstone items appeared in the national press that the new Prime Minister, Tony Blair, had turned down the two names that the Crown Appointments Commission had submitted to be the next Bishop of Liverpool, and my name was one of the two mentioned! As the whole business of Bishop's appointments in those days was meant to be kept in strict secrecy, and as I was over 60 at the time, I shrugged it off although I did not like some of the comments about me that came from rent-a-quote people the press always turn to for added colour. It was over twenty years later when I was well into retirement that I was telephoned by some ecclesiastical civil servant and told that a leak had taken place and the whole inside story of the Liverpool appointment was now in public domain. And, yes, I was the person who was turned down. I read all the conversations on the internet and I learnt that the Prime Minister's advisor, who had never met me, had strongly advised against my appointment. Again I was not considered serious enough for such a post.

So where was my Divine companion in all this? The answer, which one can see very clearly twenty years further, is that if I had been offered the post I would probably have said "yes" and that would have been the wrong choice. I was too old to take over a very challenging position (and, in fairness, the Prime Minister's advisor also said that). As it was there was plenty to do in my Maidstone position to say nothing of the fact that I was heading up the Church of England's preparations to celebrate the Millennium and that was getting to a critical stage. So I did not like the human reasons for my rejection but I can see that God was still at work in closing that door. I am also glad that I did not know about it at the time!

How then do I conclude from all that has happened in my life? It is that the one who accompanied me did not necessarily spare me from the ups and downs of life or even intervene when I made bad decisions, rather he worked with the person I was and often brought me into contact with the person I most needed at key moments - such as Dean Hatto in my college days, or the casual phrase of a friend that led me out of the wrong job, or the nervous words of a young waitress in a Norwich hotel. No I cannot point to continual dramatic experiences, but when one looks back on that time - a time that has lasted for nearly ninety years, I can only say that God has been with me - and as the psalmist said, he has been my shepherd …and "even though I walk through the valley of the shadow of death, I will fear no evil"

And Now...

So starts the famous song that Frank Sinatra made his own. It is the song of a man looking back on his life and defiantly saying that in spite of a few regrets, he was glad that he did it *my way.*

I start this final chapter with the same words but the difference is that I look back on my attempts to live my life *his way* - not, I fear, always with success on my part. Unlike the song, I have had more than a few regrets. What I want to do in the pages ahead is to share some of the lessons I have been trying to learn and to pose some of the questions I want to ask the generation of my, rather brilliant, grandchildren.

The biggest lesson is that Jesus Christ and his call to follow is what Christianity is all about. While I was Bishop of Maidstone - a junior colleague of The Archbishop of Canterbury - I remember being given a bracelet with the letters WWJD embroidered in it. The letters stood for "What would Jesus do". It was given to me by a group of young people in the Diocese. I wore it one day when I had to chair one of the many committees that modern people think is the only way to run an organisation. As we went through the agenda I kept feeling that Jesus would hardly want to do anything that we were discussing!

In my time I have sat as a child on a Sunday School

seat, and sat on a chair at a meeting of Bishops or in General Synod. The Sunday School was nearer to the heart of Christianity than either of the other places! Yes, I know that organisations need leadership and the "Church" cannot avoid being an organisation. Jesus, however, left an organisation to run an underground operation and a growing movement; our present leadership structures are sometimes hard to relate to what Jesus left behind.

Again over the centuries we have built up an imposing skyscraper of theological wisdom. All over the world universities have professor's chairs on the subject. I have learnt from some of them. Yet when the great theologian Karl Barth quoted the words of a Sunday School song on one occasion, he was at his best. The words were; *"Jesus loves me this I know, for the Bible tells me so".* The first Christians had only the memories of living with Jesus. As I noted earlier those first converts were taught by those who had lived alongside Jesus. As my ministry developed over the years I began to see that I had to stick closely to the stories and sayings of the one I felt called to follow. That does not give me an answer to every question, but it gives me enough to get on with. I try to follow the one who knows, but I will never know all that he knows.

A key moment in my own university theological training was listening to a lecturer I admired speaking about those passages in the Old Testament describing the people of Israel clearly believing that God was calling them to destroy every man woman and child in certain of their enemy communities. Today we would term that as genocide. As someone who had been encouraged to hold the Bible in high regard, this lecture was a shattering experience. I remember saying to myself 'what do I tell my

Sunday School class on Sunday?' The only thing I could hold onto then, and still do, is that Jesus is the best insight into what God is like, and genocide doesn't come into a picture where he is present. For me the Bible doesn't start with Adam and Eve - perceptive though that story is - it starts on the shore of the Sea of Galilee and that man Jesus inviting us to follow him.

A second area where I feel I have been learning, is to do with the 'gospel'. From Sunday School days and singing that lovely hymn *There is a green hill far away,* I was very clear that the gospel was all about the cross.

> 'He died that we might be forgiven
> He died to make us good
> That we might go at last to heaven
> Saved by his precious blood
>
> There was no other good enough
> To pay the price of sin;
> He only could unlock the gate
> Of heaven and let us in'

Hugely simple words and perhaps some theologians could have field day with them, but I still hold to what those verses say. They square with Christ's words at the Last Supper when he took bread and broke it in front of his followers and then said *'This is my body which is given for you. Do this to remember me.' (Luke 22.19 NLT)* It is, indeed, good news that in some profound way, Jesus died so that we who have let him down can be considered innocent in the eyes of God. St Peter wrote: *'Christ suffered for our sins, once for all time. He never sinned, but died for sinners to bring you safely home to God.' (NLT 1Peter3.18)*

All that said, Jesus speaks of a 'gospel' in another way.

When he first called those Galilean fishermen to follow him he said: *'The Kingdom of God is near! Repent of your sins and believe the Good News!' (Mark 1.15 NLT).* This was the message that his first followers believed and left their livelihoods to share. In a world, like ours, where the powers that be call us to live for selfish values - or even just to survive - Jesus was holding out the values of a better world. It was a world well summed up in his famous beatitudes. A world where those who admit their needs of God's help will prosper; where those who share the sufferings of others will find comfort; where those who are gentle will end up the clear winners in life; where those who are driven to see right and good prevail will find satisfaction, where those who show mercy to others will find mercy coming back; where those who are concentrated on these values will find that God himself is on their side; and where those who work for peace will sense they are in God's very family. And if they are persecuted for living in this way, they will know that a better day and a better world awaits them.

What we have here is a gospel of the Kingdom. The promise of a better world to come where God is truly King, but where we can work now for some of his values to be realised or approximated in our present world.
So I have come to see that there are two sides to what Jesus called the gospel, but both are held together in himself. *In fact, the gospel is Jesus!*

A third area where I have been learning lessons is to do with church differences. Christianity presents itself, at times, as a very divided (but still amazingly large) number of people. If I had stayed in Scotland I might well have ended up as a Presbyterian - and possibly as one of a fairly liberal mindset.   As it was I landed in an Anglican parish with a strongly (although not narrowly) evangelical mindset.   I might, like the man who knelt and crossed himself on my first night in the Air Force, have been born into a Catholic family and followed the family path.

After all the complications of being around for twenty centuries it is not surprising that there are now different traditions.   One of the reasons the then Prime Minister was advised to turn me down for the Liverpool Bishoprick was that I was "an out and out evangelical".   The truth is that I am someone who wants to follow Jesus first, and other labels fade in the light of that understanding. I have come to see that the various traditions of Christianity tend to "breed true" when it comes to their offspring, and they should not be "blamed" for that.   The question I have to ask myself is whether a person has said "yes" to Jesus.   The culture of saying "yes" may be different from mine, but that does not change the reality of what comes from a person's heart.

And just as that group of new recruits when I started my National Service needed to experience the joint witness of an Evangelical and a Roman Catholic, so I believe that future generations of British people will need to see the united witness of all who try to follow Jesus no matter what label is over their respective church doors.   All the evidence, as I write, is that the numbers of Christians are in steady decline and - humanly speaking - it is hard to see the decline being stopped, never mind turning to rising again. When I failed as a religious editor working for my second publishing organisation, part of the story was that, even in the early 1970s, the number of Christians was actually declining.   There were fewer readers.   As I mentioned earlier, most people turn to faith before the end of their teens with local church influence or believing parents being the main causes. The scale of children's work - compared to the 1960s - has shrunk dramatically. Children grow up and become parents themselves and if they have never found faith in Christ then their children are hardly likely to be encouraged to do so.

I can only see that the smaller numbers will shrink the scale of denominational organisations and some may even collapse. As for my own Church of England (to which I owe so much) my fear is that over the last 100 years we have moved to having very heavy central organisations - all of which cost money. My fear also is that, in any decline, the centre might be the last to allow itself to shrink. That would be wrong because our resources need to be in the local churches linked together in more flexible dioceses. The attractive agents in future Christianity will be (as it always should have been) the witness of individual Christians.

That witness will have to be in the ways of Jesus as well as his words. This leads me to another lesson I have been learning. I am an evangelist and felt called to be so. My greatest concern was that people discover Jesus for themselves and learn both about God and about how to live from him. But that begs the question of what is that "*how*" that we should be living? One of the dangers of a narrowly evangelical stance is that you want to convert people so that they then go out to convert others - end of story. Jesus however apprenticed his first followers into being more than salesmen for God. They saw that healing mattered. They saw Jesus anxious that people had enough to eat. The "gospel" Jesus demonstrated was this gospel *of the Kingdom.* He wanted people to experience a taster of the world as it will become when God will ultimately rule. Followers of Jesus today may well not be able to miraculously feed thousands from next to nothing or make the blind see, but we are called to make the world a better place - something a bit nearer to the heaven we seek. We may speak about the *gospel of the cross* but we must live out *the gospel of the Kingdom.*

That is why I rejoice in the way churches have set up such things as food banks and night shelters and work amongst the homeless, world-wide relief and development organisations, amongst many other things. It was Jesus who once challenged his followers when he said that inasmuch as we did caring things to those in need we were doing it to him.

I have also learnt that there is no perfect church - local or in denominational dimensions. How could there be? Every Sunday in church services we formally confess our sins - churches are made up of imperfect people. Yes, we may be learning to be better but every Christian should remember that they have an "L" plate on their backs - and that includes those called to be Church leaders. One thing that became clear to me as a bishop is that every organisation (including churches) is a subtle conspiracy against other organisations! A leader is always under the temptation to exonerate what his or her organisation is doing, or has done. In recent years that became plain with child abuse claims against clergy. I use the phrase 'in recent years' because society at large has only just woken up, in the last thirty years, to the reality and horridness of child abuse. I am sure that it has always been going on where adults mix with children. Much attention has been focussed on church failings, but two things need to be made clear. There have always been people with paedophile tendencies and such people have always been drawn to mix with children whether it be in churches or in movements like the Boy Scouts or even in schools themselves. The problem is not churches but, first and foremost, paedophiles themselves.

The second thing is that society at large has only just woken up to the horrific damage that people suffer not just through being abused but for years afterwards. In my early years as a minister one heard about the odd Choirmaster or Sunday School teacher who was 'over familiar' with children. The usual response was that such a person was dismissed (often in an undemonstrative manner) and life went on. This left the abused child often without counsel and the offender ready to find new targets elsewhere. In Britain it was the *Children Act* that brought things out into the open. When one heard of an offence the Police had to be informed. I remember one case where a young priest went to see the Diocesan counsellor to ask for help with his inordinate feelings towards his step-daughter only to be told "Will you go to the police or shall I?"

In the Church of England we now have teams of people in every Diocese charged with "Safeguarding". I think we need to have something like this but the danger is that we can move into a culture where suspicions are reported, which have to be examined, and yet often are proved to be without foundation. In such cases damage is done to the wrong people. I remember a Diocesan Bishop being suspended from duties while Safeguarding practices were pursued, only to have to pick up the pieces later when he was "cleared" of what was never there in the first place.

As I write the biggest issue that the churches have been facing has been to do with sex and marriage.   For generations the nation took its lead on these matters from the Church, now the nation is waiting for the churches to catch up - or so it feels.   Our society approves of same sex marriages and, rightly, consenting homosexuals are no longer considered to be criminals.   There are many gay and lesbian people who deeply feel that those who name the name of Jesus have let them down badly.   All through my ministry there has been a controversy over same sex relationships, and the arrival of AIDS on the scene in the 1980s brought the issue into sharp focus.   I wrote a book, at that time, called *Beyond Aids* - and I wish I had not.   It is one of my regrets.   It spelled out a conservative position but with little proper awareness that much of what I said would have caused pain - not least to those who were dying from the illness.

The conservative arguments draw from several references in the Bible and from a clear argument about what was in the Creator's mind when, as the book of Genesis says, *"male and female he created them"* (Genesis 1.27).   Our very anatomies suggest that heterosexuality was intended to be normative.   The trouble with leaving the arguments at this point, however, is that *genuine human love is always more than sexual engagements.*   Perhaps behind the modern nature of the controversy, is the tacit assumption that sexual gratification is the human right of every person.   I do not believe that to be the case.

To go back to my conviction that the key to our understanding has to be based on what Jesus said or did, there is nothing in the gospel accounts that sheds any light on the issue one way or another. And Jesus lived without seeking sexual gratification.

For decades this issue has been presented as a controversy. A controversy means that two sides are battling to gain victory over the other. Until I retired the Church of England was clearly the victor over the arguments and pressure of the gay and lesbian community. However it should never have been like that and I am ashamed that I saw myself on the winner's side. In the last twenty years, however, the tide has turned. Gay marriages are part of the law of the land. There are many in the churches calling for a total reversal of old attitudes. I came to the view, since retirement, that all the dynamics of controversy were wrong. *The issue should have been seen as a dilemma not a controversy.* In a dilemma you may have two "sides" but they are both partners in the dilemma. Both sides have to present their case - even passionately. Both sides also have to have sympathy for those who feel they have to differ.. Today after all the hostility perceived to come from the conservative proponents the new victors sometimes reflect that hostility back. One of the dynamics of the so-called "woke" viewpoint is not only a championing of what were minority opinions, but a cancelling out of those who challenge such views. As gay acceptability becomes the norm, there needs to be a generous acceptance of those of us who still see that heterosexuality was seen to be the norm in what our Creator has given the human race.

This brings me to the question of marriage. I think our society is in a muddle on this matter. I mentioned earlier that I had to encounter "unmarried" parents presenting babies for baptism. I found that such parents had no intention of separating. I believe that more children are being born in Britain out of wedlock rather than within it.   Why are people rejecting marriage?   The answer is complex but rarely shameful.

It has become a widespread view that "marriage" is a Christian institution.   It is not - ask a Muslim!   Then there are also some people championing the view that "Civil Partnerships" should be favoured to "marriage". Their view seems to be that in marriage the woman is subordinate to the man.   I believe this view is wrong but there are some grounds for holding such a mistaken position.   The traditional Prayer Book wedding has a place where the priest asks "who gives this woman to be married to this man".   At this point the father of the bride is supposed to indicate that he is handing over the bride.   The service also asks the bride whether she will "obey" her new husband.   I think both of these things go back to previous cultural situations where - way back - a woman's security was left to being related to men who could protect against other men.   This was certainly so in Biblical times.   This virtual subordination of the woman is also to be found in some religious cultures including some brands of Christianity.   However I love the use of the word "partners" in the phrase "civil partnership", but the model for British civil partnership between two adults of the same sex was taken from the concept of marriage. I know that St Paul said some pretty strong statements regarding women in marriage but careful searching of his words show that he also talked about the equal value of the wife.   He was writing to the first Christian converts who were living in paternalistic cultures and some of what he said to woman converts reflected on how they had to live with unconverted husbands.   For me marriage is always about being partners together.   St Peter said of the wife (to chauvinistic readers) that *"she is your equal partner in God's gift of new life".* (1 Peter 3.7 NLT)

My problem with marriages today relates to the clutter that seems to be attached to getting married. There are plenty of cohabiting couples who have no intention of splitting up and many have children. Why are they not married? For quite a few there is the view that "they don't need a bit of paper" to live together. I remember speaking about this in General Synod back in 1992! I argued that most cohabiting couples actually fulfilled the Biblical criteria for being married. The trouble is that we have overlaid those Biblical requirements with cultural (and some legal) additions. The cultural things - including the vast intrusions of the wedding industry and expensive receptions and stag and hen parties - do put many off "getting married". The legal things, however, are important. Society at large needs to know where it stands with regard to human partnerships - especially when it comes to children and property . I wonder whether we could do things more simply. What, I wonder, could happen if a couple signed, with witnesses, a form declaring that they intended to be partners together for the rest of their lives - and for this to be centrally recorded? Such a requirement might well be welcomed by couples who had already lived together for a few years, and have children, but would baulk at the present formalities of "getting married".

What then are the questions I want to ask of the generation which includes my brilliant grandchildren. They are the questions of an old man who is *still believing.*

My first question would be: *what community are you living in?* I live fairly near a school and the thing I notice is that as soon as children leave the premises, out come the smart phones. Whenever I go out to a restaurant I usually see a family group around another table and half of them (usually the younger half) are looking at their phones. A common complaint of singers and groups at concerts is that they are confronted by a sea of phones - recording what they do for another time. I have tried to steer clear of the so-called "social-media" although I am caught up in a *whats app* group. I think the trouble with such groups is that expression is too close to one's immediate mental reactions. By that I mean that one very easily puts on record exactly the first thought one gets - but first thoughts are rarely the thoughts that are the best. First thoughts are often very close to feelings - even raw feelings. The trouble is that once one taps the button, one's perhaps ill-considered reaction is now " on the record". One of the complaints I hear about is that social media can become the vehicle for nastiness. "Trolling" it is called. Suicides have even been encouraged or contemplated from someone being caught up in persistent trolling.

And the trouble with expressing anger is that it can release one into further expressions of anger. In normal physical interaction, one angry comment can often bring an angry reaction, and that can be sobering . It can remind you that words hurt and that you are dealing with a person. The problem with trolling is that one does not get the immediate reaction - one can hurt without getting hurt back.

I sometimes wonder whether internet media anger lies behind the frequent reports that people seem to insult each other more in recent years. Football referees at amateur and youth matches are beginning to get body cameras fitted to record what players, coaches and parents say to them. Doctors' surgery reception areas often carry notices warning against insulting behaviour. The world of smartphones is one where we are being encouraged to react rather than reflect. It also discourages us to live in the present with the information that immediately surrounds us.

My second question is the question that was put to the professor I mentioned earlier: *why is there anything?* Of course evolution has played a part in the shaping of our world - but as I said earlier, evolution needs something to begin with - even if it is a primordial soup. The reason I ask myself and others this question is that we have a choice to make as to why we are here. Either we are the result of a series of accidents or there we are here by some sort of design. If we are satisfied with the answer of "accidents" then there would seem to be no reason why we should not live in a totally random manner, and , at best, any morality we have grasped is a personal choice. Should I hurt other people then why not - unless one guesses that other people might hurt us back. Orderly society comes about when the majority of people agree to certain rules - sometimes because those rules are being imposed by those in some alpha position.

There are plenty of people in our world who believe in "good" and "bad" and who try to live their lives in the light of such judgments. Mind you, this can be regional. The consensus of what is good and bad can change dramatically from place to place. In my country it is illegal to marry more than one person, but that is not so in some other parts of the world. My overriding point, however, is that all these things come from minds who have to admit they are the result of meaningless accidents. To repeat what I said earlier, one of our most famous philosophers simply said "the universe just is, that's all we can say!". That means that everything is, ultimately, unexplainable.

So my question to my grandchildren's generation is are you satisfied with this? My guess is that many who would say that they are intellectually satisfied with this conclusion, would nevertheless live as if life had some sort of meaning and that words like "right" and "good" and "bad" and even "love" makes sense. And thank God they do.

My final question takes me back to a trip in a London minicab about twenty years ago. The driver, who I guessed was Turkish, asked me what I did for a living. I said I was a Christian minister, and he was immediately interested. God, he said , meant a great deal to him. It was clear that he was a Moslem but when that had been established in our conversation, he then asked the killer question. *"How much do you know about Islam?"* I said that I had a copy of the Koran and had read bits of it. We chatted and as we parted he took an attractively presented booklet out of his glove drawer, and gave it to me. I read it later. It didn't try to convert me, rather it simply set out the the central beliefs of Islam.

That set me thinking - not least as someone who many years ago published books and booklets about Christianity. So the question I would want to ask my grandchildren's generation is "how much do you know about Jesus Christ? I wouldn't want to use the word "Christianity" because that term get bogged down under the weight of buildings and dressed up clergy and the history of crusades to say nothing of scandals of child abuse. I do not want to appear to be trying to convert, for the simple reason that people need to know what it is that they are being asked to convert to. I really do not believe that many people outside the churches really know about Jesus, and they are joined by quite a few inside the churches also!

I often wonder how many of those who say they do not believe in Christianity have ever read the gospel accounts. They are not very long. Our modern minds might find parts of the story strange. One is thrown into a world where miracles happen (although not as often as one might imagine). One reads accounts of Jesus written by his contemporaries who think the world is flat; and yet none of this - I believe - stops a picture coming through that makes one look towards a better world. And what one sees is this man's effect on a group of fairly normal people that makes them feel that they have to change their plans and follow Him, even if the rest of society deems them to be stupid. As I said earlier, Jesus did not ask for a bit of their time. He wanted all of it.

Those men and women believed their future would be in a better world, and tried to make their present world more like the world to come. They "learned Jesus" and I cannot think of a better way to live. I am still near the bottom of the class in that learning, and I wish I had been a better follower, but the biggest thing about Jesus is that he is a forgiver. I am trusting in that.

I close by going back to what I said earlier about receiving a letter from an unknown man in Canada asking me to come and address some meetings in Toronto. When I agreed to this unknown person he said that if I reported to the Air Canada desk at Heathrow Airport I would find a ticket and board the plane to Toronto. I had no advance proof that this was not a hoax, but I trusted in what I had been told, and did what I was asked to do - and by doing that found that it was all true and - amongst other things - had gained a lifelong friend.

If I was to be asked about Jesus by anyone in my grandchildren's generation, I would say start reading the stories about him by those who lived beside him, and assume that they are true, and set out to try to follow him as his first followers did. And as you do so share your thoughts and fears with him believing he can somehow hear, and trust that in one way or another he will keep showing up as an unseen helper. And if you feel a failure remember that he forgave the very people who tried to kill him.

And if you do these things, you will get to the end of your lives *still believing.*

My Prayer At The Start Of The Day

Thank you Father for wanting me to be
Alive and for the gift of this day
May I honour you in the hours to come

Thank you Lord Jesus, rescuer and friend,
For calling me to follow you,
May you be seen in me today

Thank you Holy Spirit for promising
to be with me
All through this day and all through my life
May I never forget that promise

Amen

Printed in Great Britain
by Amazon

25067874R00057